D'Arcy W. Thompson

Ancient Leaves

Or translations and paraphrases from poets of Greece and Rome

D'Arcy W. Thompson

Ancient Leaves
Or translations and paraphrases from poets of Greece and Rome

ISBN/EAN: 9783337380472

Printed in Europe, USA, Canada, Australia, Japan

Cover: Foto ©Thomas Meinert / pixelio.de

More available books at **www.hansebooks.com**

OR

TRANSLATIONS AND PARAPHRASES FROM
POETS OF GREECE AND ROME

BY

D'ARCY W. THOMPSON

Novas frondes et non sua poma

EDINBURGH

EDMONSTON AND DOUGLAS

1862

TRANSLATIONS.

PARAPHRASES.

ERRATUM.

Page 27, line 12, *instead of.*

I and child put on the yoke of slaves,

read,

I and thy child put on the yoke of slaves.

AJAX.

———◆———

CHARACTERS OF THE PLAY.

ATHENE (Minerva).   TEUCER, half-brother of Ajax.

AJAX, prince of Salamis.   AGAMEMNON, king of Mycenæ.

ULYSSES, king of Ithaca.   MENELAUS, king of Sparta.

TECMESSA, wife of Ajax.   A MESSENGER.

Chorus of Salaminian Sailors.

SILENT CHARACTERS.

EURYSACES, son of Ajax.   The TUTOR of EURYSACES.   HERALD.

SCENE I.

Exterior of the tent of AJAX.   ULYSSES *enters, looking*
cautiously around; ATHENE *speaks from mid-air,*
supposed to be invisible from the stage.

Ath. Son of Laertes, ever have I known thee

Upon thy foeman's track a hunter keen;

So now upon the sea-beach near the tent

B

Of Ajax, where he holds the outmost post,

This while past have I seen thee trace and mark

His new-imprinted footsteps, to discover

Whether the hero be within or no :

Thy steps are sure as scent of Spartan hound ;

It was but now he went within, his face

Reeking with sweat and his hands red with blood.

So, come, thou need'st not peer within the gate,

But freely speak thine errand out, and one,

Who knoweth all, will speed thee on thy way.

  Ulys. Dearest Athene, though unseen the while,

Yet well known is that voice, as loud and clear

As the deep note of a Tyrrhenian bell.

Thou seest me on the traces of a foe,

Ajax, the bearer of the seven-fold shield.

For but this night past he hath done a deed

Most passing strange—if that the deed be his ;

For herein we are all at fault, and I

Have set myself to find this riddle out.

This morning to our wonder we beheld

All slain and mangled most inhumanly

Our flocks and herds, shepherds and herdsmen, all :

The deed was of man's doing, and that deed

The general voice doth lay at this man's door.

Ay, and a scout, seeing him all alone

With dripping sword go bounding o'er the plain,

Thereof informs me, and on the moment I

Rush in pursuit, and ever and anon

Methinks I see my way, then comes a check,

And straightway am I all at fault again.

But thou art come most seasonably ; and now,

As heretofore, thy hand shall be my guide.

  Ath. I know it all ; and, knowing all, I came

To see thee safely through thy perilous chase.

  Ulys. Tell me, dear Mistress, do I toil in vain ?

  Ath. Nay, nay; the deed was all of this man's

    doing.

  Ulys. What earthly purpose for so strange a deed ?

  Ath. 'Twas done in anger, that Achilles' arms

Were given to thee ?

Ulys.   But, prithee, wherefore, Goddess,
Turn'd he his hand against the innocent herd ?

Ath. 'Twas in your blood he thought to dye his hands.

Ulys. The deed was meant for us ?

Ath.   Was meant, and would
Have had successful issue, but for me.

Ulys. How set about a task so terrible ?

Ath. Against you he came stealing in the dark,
Alone.

Ulys.   And came he near his journey's end ?

Ath. He had reached the tent-doors of the brother
             kings.

Ulys. And how restrained he then his murderous
             hand ?

Ath. I held him back, and placed before his eyes
Unreal visions of delirium born,
And turned his steps to where the herdsmen watch'd
The undivided booty of the host :
On these he fell, and pêle-mêle, right and left,
He slew and hack'd the hornèd throng, and now

The two Atridæ fall beneath his hand,

Now this, and now another of the kings.

I all the while to fiercer frenzy goad

The madman on, and make the mischief worse.

And, when at length he rested from his toil,

The living remnants of the flocks and herds

He bound, and drave before him to his tent

Oxen and sheep, as men, his prisoners.

And now within the tent he scourgeth them.

But I will shew thee this same madman's work,

That thou may'st see and tell it to thy friends.

Stay ; never fear ; he cannot do thee harm ;

I will so turn his eyes, he shall not see,

Although thou stand before him face to face.

Ho ! thou that bindest fast thy prisoners' hands,

Ajax, come forth !

    Ulys.   What ? call the man out here ?

    Ath. Hush, sirrah ; shew thy manhood.

    Ulys.   Nay, let him be ;

By heaven, I am content he stay within.

Ath. For fear of what? was Ajax more than
man?

Ulys. He was, as he is still, mine enemy.

Ath. What laugh so sweet as at a foe's expense?

Ulys. Howbeit, I had rather he should stay
within.

Ath. Upon a madman art afraid to look?

Ulys. Were he not mad, then were I not afraid.

Ath. I tell thee yet again he shall not see.

Ulys. What? sees he not with the same eyes as
ever?

Ath. Those eyes shall see, yet, while they see, be
blind.

Ulys. Well, well; the rough is smooth, if Gods
so will it.

Ath. Stand still, and wait.

Ulys.　　　　　　　Well—as thou bidst—I stay:
(*Aside*) But would to heaven I were a league away.

Ath. Ajax—a second time I call thee forth—
This is scant courtesy to so old a friend.

(*Enter* AJAX *from the tent.*)

Ajax. All hail, Athene ! welcome, child of Zeus !

Thou comest in season : for this booty here

I will repay thee with a crown of gold.

    Ath. Well said, my friend ; but, prithee, tell me

         first,—

Thy sword, was it well steep'd in Argive blood ?

    Ajax. Ay, Goddess, ay.

    Ath.   And did'st thou turn thy hands

Against the kings?

    Ajax.   It will be long before

Ajax meets insult at their hands again.

    Ath. The kings are dead then? so thy words imply.

    Ajax. Ay, dead, and free to rob me of mine arms.

    Ath. Good : and how far'd it with Laertes' son ?

Hath he escaped ?

    Ajax.   The subtle, scheming knave ?

    Ath. I mean Ulysses, who supplanted thee.

Ajax. He sits fast-bound within, a sight to feast
Mine eyes withal—he dies not yet awhile.

   Ath. Not yet awhile? why, what would'st thou do
        more?

   Ajax. I'll bind him to the pillar of my tent,
And lash and flay his bare back till he die.

   Ath. Be not so stern, I pray thee, with the wretch.

   Ajax. Athene, in all else I will give way,
But here my will is fixed; the man dies so.

   Ath. Well, if it be thy pleasure so to do,
Lay on with a will, and wreak thy vengeance out.

   Ajax. I go; but, ere I go, one thing I pray;
Be to me evermore the friend thou art to-day.

                       (Exit)

   Ath. See'st thou, Ulysses, what the Gods can do?
Did'st ever know a man more wise than this,
Or stouter-hearted in the hour of need?

   Ulys. Not one: and in good sooth I pity him,
Poor man, altho' he is mine enemy,
Seeing him mated with a fate so hard;

For his chance serves as mirror to mine own,

And now I see that we poor men are made

Of dream-stuff, the mere shadows of a shade.

 Ath. Seeing these things, remember that thou speak

No word of insolence against the Gods,

Nor boast thyself, if that thy neighbour's hand

Be weaker, or his substance less than thine :

Time bringeth low and raiseth up again

All human things, and the great Gods above

Abhor the wicked, as the good they love.

(Exeunt.)

Chorus. (*Recitative.*)

Son of Telamon from sea-girt Salamis : I rejoice me in
  thy prosperity ;

But when the wrath of Zeus or slanderous tongues
  assail thee : I quake and tremble like a fluttering
  dove.

Even so this night past we have heard : dreadful
  stories to thy shame ;

How thou wentest to the pasture-grounds : and slewest
the cattle and the flocks;

Hewing with thy shining sword : all the remnant of
the prey.

Such words of slander doth Ulysses : whisper in the
ears of all;

And all are easy of belief : for the words he speaketh
have the shew of truth;

And the hearer rejoiceth more in thy sorrow : than the
teller of the tales;

For whoso aimeth at the great ones of the earth : he
shall not miss his mark;

For envy is the heritage of the rich : but the arrow
glanceth from the side of the lowly.

Princes and people asunder : are even as a tottering
tower;

But herein there is safety : when they lean one upon
the other;

These are words for the wise : for a fool cannot learn
them betimes.

So men cry against thee, O king : and we alone are
  weak to resist ;

For so soon as they are out of thy sight : they clamour
  like a flock of birds ;

But if the eagle should come suddenly : they would
  cower down in terror, and be dumb.

STROPHE. (*Aria.*)

Did Tauric Artemis, the child of Zeus

(O dreadful story, mother of my shame)

Turn thee against the booty of the host,

Angry, because in battle or the chase

She lack'd due honour at thy hands ?

Or, jealous of thee, his rival in the fight,

Did the brazen War-God in revenge

Put thee to shame in the watches of the night ?

ANTISTROPHE.

For never of thyself could'st thou have gone astray

So far as to fall upon the herds :

The malady is sent from heaven ;

But may Zeus and Apollo avert slanderous tongues.

And if the great chiefs and the Ithacan accurs'd

Secretly speak words of ill,

Make not the evil worse by sitting still, O king,

And sullenly brooding in thy tent by the sea.

EPODE.

Nay, rise from where thou sittest,

These many days resting from the troubles of the war,

And heaping fresh wrath from heaven upon thine head ;

And the triumph of thy foes rageth unchecked,

As a fire rageth in the sheltered dells ;

And the babbling words they utter are a burden to
    the ear ;

And this is all sad, sad to me.

(*Enter* TECMESSA.)

Tecm. Sailors of Ajax, children of the race

Of earthborn old Erectheus, 'tis for us

To mourn and weep, for us and all that love

The house of Telamon beyond the seas.

For now my lord, the great broad-shoulder'd Ajax,

Lies overwhelm'd beneath a sea of troubles.

   Chor. What burden fresh, to yesterday unknown,

Hath night brought with it? speak, Phrygian lady, speak :

Thou, erst the spoil of war to our great lord,

Art now his well-beloved wife : so speak ;

Thou needs must know all we so fain would hear.

   Tecm. O how to tell the tale unutterable !

Listen : 't will chill thy very life to hear :

Ajax, our own great Ajax, this night past

Went mad ; aye, mad ; to his peril and his shame.

Within his tent here you may see a heap

Of mangled carcases, welt'ring in blood ;

And these are all the victims of his hand.

CHORUS. (*Recitative.*)

Thou givest sad tidings of our brave hero : of sorrows

    hard to bear ; sorrows hard to shun ;

The chieftains bruit the story abroad : and Rumour
    swelleth the words as they fly.

The gleaming sword was in his frenzied hand : when
    he slew the cattle and the herdsmen ;

I fear me what the morrow will bring forth : for the
    penalty of such things is death.

    Tecm. Ah ! now I see whence came the fleecy crowd
Of prisoners he drove this morning home ;
One he chose out, and slew upon the ground ;
Others he hacked or rent in twain ; and two
White-footed rams he lifted one by one,
And from the first he cut the head and tongue,
And flung them on the ground ; then took the other,
And laid on blows with a great, sounding thong,
With awful words, such as the Gods teach men
Then only when they push them on to ruin.

        CHORUS. (*Recitative.*)

Now were it time to veil our faces : and to steal
    away unseen ;

Or seated on the benches of a swift-sailing ship : to
    trust to the winds and sea.

For the brothers, who are lords of the host : speak
    threatening words against us ;

To stone us with stones, both us and our king : our
    king frenzy-stricken of the Gods.

    Tecm. No longer so ; for as the wind that blows

With lightning unaccompanied from the South

Suddenly falls, and leaves the heaven serene ;

So fares it with him now ; but in the lull

Fresh sorrows crowd upon him, and the sight

Of all this havoc due to his hand alone

Doth wound him to the quick.

    Chor.   Nay, lady, nay ;

If it be so, all may e'en yet go well ;

The cause removed, ill words will die away.

    Tecm. If choice were given thee, whether wouldst
              thou choose

Paining thy friends to be at ease thyself,

Or share with them their sorrow.

Chor.   Surely, dear lady,
The double sorrow were the greater ill.

    Tecm. Just so our cure hath wrought us misery.

    Chor. Thou speak'st in riddles; prithee, make
           them plain.

    Tecm. The hero yonder, while the craze was on him,
Himself drew comfort from his sad estate,
And we, whose wits were clear, had all the pain;
Now that the respite from disease is come,
He is bow'd down with agony and shame,
And ours is but a poor gain by the change:
Is not this making troubles twain of one?

    Chor. Even so, lady; and therefore I do fear
This blow is sent from heaven; else how should he,
From madness freed, be still the slave of sorrow?

    Tecm. It is too late for "I do fear :" the thing
Needs now "I know."

    Chor.   How came it at the first?
Tell us, who take thy sorrow for our own.

    Tecm. Thou shalt hear all; thy lot is one with ours;

It was the dead of night, and all the lamps

Of evening were gone out, when he up-rose,

Girt on his great sword, and on tip-toe crept

To the tent-door upon his lonely way.

And chiding him I said, " What may this mean,

Ajax ? upon what errand art thou bound ?

No herald's voice hath summon'd thee, or call

Of trumpet : nay, the whole host is asleep."

And he with the old proverb made reply ;

" A woman's chiefest grace is a still tongue ;"

I answer'd not, and he went out alone;

And what he did out there I cannot tell,

But back he came, driving a throng before him

Of oxen, shepherd-dogs, and horned goats;

From some he smote the heads ; some he held back,

And cut across the throat ; some down the chine ;

Some he bound fast, and rail'd and struck at them,

The silly sheep, as they were mortal men.

And at the last he issued out of doors,

And with some fancied creature of the brain

In boastful words held converse of the kings,

Th' Atreidæ and Ulysses, laughing the while

At all the vengeance that he held in store ;

Then came indoors, where by most slow degrees,

Little and little his poor wits came back :

But, when the horror all around grew clear,

He struck his forehead, and shriek'd aloud, and fell

Down in amongst the weltering carcases ;

And there he sat, with his hair clench'd in both hands.

So for a while he sat without a word,

Then burst he out into most awful threats,

Unless I told him the whole story out,

And let him know the case, wherein he stood.

And I, my friends, in terror told him all,

All, that I knew ; and straightway he burst out

Into a groan, the like of which I ne'er

Had heard before from him ; for he was wont

To reckon such the mark of a mean soul :

And so with him 'twas no shrill cry, but a groan

Stilled, like the low bellowing of a bull.

And now in his most utter misery,

Without or food or drink, the man is sitting

Speechless, with the heap'd carcases around.

But in the words half-heard amid his groans

I read the import of some stern resolve.

Wherefore, my friends, I am come forth to beg

Your help, if any help can now avail ;

For men like him yield, if they yield, to friends.

Chor.   Child of Teleutas, this is most sad to hear ;

His crosses must have driven the poor man mad.

Ajax (*from within*).   Oh !   Oh !

Tecm.   Sad? 't will be sadder soon ; hear ye the cry,

That issues from his tent.

(AJAX *cries again from within.*)

Chor.   He is either mad,

Or stung with memory of his former madness.

Ajax (*within*).   My son !   My son !

Tecm.   Alas ! Eurysaces, he calls for thee ;

What can he mean?—where art thou child? ah me !

   ah me !

Ajax (within.) Teucer! where's Teucer? will he
       stay for ever

Upon the road, and leave me here to die?

Chor.   There's method in these words; quick, ope
       the door;

May be, the sight of us may bring him round.

Tecm.   See, then; this door I ope, for you to see
Ajax's handiwork and misery.

      (The tent-curtain is drawn aside, and AJAX
       is seen seated amid a heap of slain cattle;
       a ram is fastened to the tent-pillar.)

(AJAX *singing*).

    O messmates dear, of many friends
       Faithful among the faithless found;
      See what a surging tide of blood
       Circles me round, circles me round.

Chor.   Alas, alas; thy words are all too true;
To have come to this, thou hast been mad indeed.

Ajax.   O comrades! mine on land or sea,
       Loyal to your master still;

For pity's sake your aid forbear :

    Help not, but kill ; help not, but kill.

Chor.   Hush, hush, the cure were worse than the

    disease.

Ajax.   See here ; the valiant, the stout-hearted

    Ajax,

The foremost ever in the fight, hath spent

His might so terrible on these poor beasts—

O Gods, to think what laughter has been theirs.

Tecm.   O my lord Ajax ; prithee, speak not so.

Ajax.   Out of my sight ; quick, woman, get thee

    gone.

O me ! O me !

Chor.   Nay, never let thy sorrows master thee.

Ajax.   Me miserable ! I let the villains go,

And on the hornèd kine and bleating sheep

I fell, and dyed my hands red, red with blood.

Chor.   But wherefore grieve o'er what is past and

    gone ?

What's done cannot be undone.

Ajax.   Son of Laertes, thou whose eye and hand

Are ever busy, where mischief is at work,

Thou sorry knave, thou must have laugh'd, methinks,

Have laugh'd a laugh—ah me ! how long and sweet.

 Chor.   'Tis as heaven wills, that we or laugh or weep.

 Ajax.   Would God I saw him, even in my low

   estate !

O me !   O me !

 Chor.   Consider well, and curb these swelling

   thoughts.

 Ajax.   Sire of my sires, great Zeus, grant me the life

Of this one villain and the brother kings,

And I will die content.

 Tecm.   When thus thou prayest, pray that I die too ;

For what were life to me, when thou wert gone ?

 Ajax.   O darkness, my light,

O Erebus, most dazzling bright to me,

Take me, take me to your dwelling-place,

O take me ! on the race of Gods or men

Wherefore should I gaze longer, or what good

Could thence accrue to either them or me ?

Nay, nay ; the warrior daughter of great Zeus

Houndeth me on thro' contumely to ruin.

Where can I tarry ? whither can I flee ?

My former services are blotted out

By these misdoings ; and these silly beasts

Hang on me like a load, and the host will rise

Even as one man and slay me with their hands.

    Tecm.   O wretched me, to hear a good man say

The words he would have scorned in times gone by.

    Ajax.   O streams, that run into the sea,

Sea-caves, and pastures fringèd by the shore,

Long, long, and far too long in Trojan land

Ye've held me, but ye hold me back no longer

A living man—(*aside*) this word is for the wise.

O river, that flowest with friendly waters near,

Scamander, thou shalt never look again

On me, whose like—presumptuous words, but true—

Thy land ne'er saw in all the host that came

From Hellas ; and behold what I am now.

Chor.   Sad as thy fate is, I must needs say, Yea ;
Sad tho' thy fate be, I would fain say, Nay.

    Ajax.   Who would have thought my luckless name,
                   Aias,
To such good purpose jingled with Alas :
Aias—not once, but twice and thrice Alas !
So miserable am I ; I, whose sire,
When he had won in fight the foremost place
Among his fellows, went with glory home ;
And I, his son, who came to this same land,
With just as proud and gallant an array,
And with my good sword won as fair a fame,
Dishonour'd by the Greeks am left to die.
Yet this much will I venture ; if in life
The best and bravest had Achilles named,
And giv'n his arms as valour's meet reward,
That prize none other would have won than I,
But now th' Atreidæ play into the hands
O' the man from Ithaca, and Ajax is past by—
Ah ! had not hands and eyes and brain distraught

Swerved from my purpose, never, nevermore

Would they have sat false judges on another—

But, as my sword was stretching forth to slay,

There came Athênê, stern, invincible,

And with delusions turn'd my hand astray

To reek itself in this ignoble blood ;

And they are laughing now, out of harm's way ;

Sore, sore against my will ; but, if Heav'n will it,

The coward shall escape the better man.

And now what must I do ? I, whom the Gods

Plainly abhor, and every Greek detests,

I, whom Troy hates, and all the plains around ?

What ? shall I leave the camp upon the shore,

And o'er th' Ægean waters seek my home ;

Nay, nay ; what eyes, what forehead could I shew

My father Telamon ? would he endure

To see me coming naked of the prize

And crown of glory, that himself had won ?

This cannot be : then shall I go alone

To the walls of Troy, and fall upon the foe,

And do some noble deed before I die ?

But that, methinks, would glad the Grecian kings ;

That cannot be : some way, then, must I find

To prove to my old father, Telamon,

That I—I, Ajax—am no recreant son.

O 'tis a shame to wish for length of days,

When length of days brings with it only sorrow ;

For how can one, day after day, delight

In hanging pendulous 'twixt life and death ?

I would not value at a straw the man

That warm'd his heart with vain and silly hopes :

Nay, either noble life or noble death

Becomes the brave :—now ; I have said my say.

    Chor.   No one will charge thee with a double

                tongue,

Ajax ; these words come from thy very heart.

But lay aside these melancholy thoughts,

Let those who love thee conquer thy resolve.

    Tecm.   O my lord Ajax, there is not on earth

A power more terrible than Destiny ;

For I was born of a most noble house ;

My sire was wealthiest of Phrygian lords ;

And now I am a slave : so willed it Heav'n,

And thy right hand : wherefore, e'er since the day

I was thy wife, have I been dutiful ;

And I beseech thee by the hearth-god Zeus,

And by the bonds that make us man and wife,

Suffer it not that I should bear reproach,

A helpless captive in thine enemy's hand.

For on the day thou diest, that self-same day

Be sure that, seiz'd on by some Argive chief,

I and child put on the yoke of slaves.

And many an one o' the chieftains will then speak

These words of bitterness ; " Behold the wife

Of Ajax, once the mightiest of the host ;

Ah ! what a change for her 'twixt now and then !"

So will they speak ; and sorrow will be my lot,

And this will be for shame to thee and thine.

But leave not thy father in his sad, old age,

Leave not thy poor old mother, who many a time

Prays to the Gods to bring thee back safe home.

And, O my lord, take pity on thy son ;

Think, if he lose thy care and pass his youth

Under unfriendly guardians, what a lot,

How sad a lot thou leavest him and me.

For I have naught whereunto I may look,

Save thee : thou did'st destroy my native land ;

Father and mother, both are dead and gone ;

Where can I find a home save in thine arms ?

Thou art my father, mother, all in all —

Forget me not then ; how can a man forget

The woman he hath once clasp'd to his heart ;

Love merits love ; and he who says not so,

Is neither gallant soldier nor true man.

Chor. Had'st thou as much of pity in thy heart
As I, thou wouldst give heed to her request.

Ajax. O I will give her heed enough, if she
Will do my bidding.

Tecm. Speak and I obey.

Ajax. Bring me my child, and let me see his face.

Tecm. 'Twas fear that made me take the lad

    away.   *(hesitating.)*

Ajax. Fear of this mischief?

Tecm.   Ay, for fear, poor child,

He met with thee, and fell beneath thine hand.

    Ajax. Ay, ay, 'twere well in keeping with the

    rest.

Tecm. 'Twas to prevent it, that I took this care.

Ajax. It was well done; thy forethought I ap-

    prove.

Tecm. Is there ought left whereby to please my

    lord?

Ajax. My child, my child, let me but see my

    child.

Tecm. Thy child is close at hand, and in safe

    keeping.

Ajax. Then, woman, why is the lad so long

    a-coming?

Tecm. Thy father calls thee child—*(to a slave)* go,

    fetch him here.

Ajax (after a pause).   Well? is the slave thou
            biddest lame or deaf?

Teem.   Nay, look, here comes the slave bringing
            the boy.

Ajax.   Bring him in, bring him in hither : he will
            not fear,

Methinks, to look upon the sight of blood,

If he be truly his own father's son.

Nay, see to it, and break him in betimes,

            [To the Chorus.

And mould him after his rough father's ways.

(Enter the slave with EURYSACES : AJAX, *embracing his*
                son, continues.)

Ah, child, may'st thou be happier than thy father ;

Like in all else, and thou wilt be no coward.

And yet I cannot, child, but envy thee,

That thou art all unconscious of these woes,

For life is sweetest, when we think the least,

Or ere we know what ' joy ' and ' sorrow ' mean.

But when it comes to this, see that thou shew

Among thine enemies who thy father was.

Meanwhile enjoy all innocent delights

Of childhood, and be a comfort to thy mother.

No Greek shall harm thee with reproachful words,

Though I be absent ; such a trusty guard

Is Teucer, whom I leave, tho' now he seems

To linger far away, chasing the foe.

And you, my comrades, this I bid you all,

Tell Teucer, that he see the lad safe home

To Eribæa and to Telamon,

To be the stay and comfort of their age.

And let no chief, nor that cursed Ithacan,

Assign my arms in prizes to the host.

But thou, Eurysaces, take thou the shield,

Thy namesake—seven-fold, broad, impregnable—

The rest shall Teucer lay with me i' the grave.

But now, be quick, and take the boy away ;

And close the door, and raise no cries without—

These women are ever ready with their tears—

Shut, and be quick : it shews no skilful leech

To mutter spells o'er wounds that need the knife.

    Chor. (*aside*) I fear these sharp words and this

               eager haste.

    Tecm. O my lord Ajax what is this thy will ?

    Ajax. Ask not, but shew thy sense by a still

               tongue.

    Tecm. Ah me ! how sad my heart is — O by thy

               child,

And by the Gods I pray thee leave us not.

    Ajax. Thou plaguest me ; why, what owe I the

               Gods,

That I for their sakes should be bounden to thee ?

    Tecm. Hush, hush, my lord.

    Ajax.   Go, speak to ears that hear.

    Tecm. Thou wilt not yield then ?

    Ajax.   Wilt thou speak for ever ?

    Tecm. My fears would for me.

    Ajax.   Take her away forthwith.

    Tecm. For Heaven's sake listen.

Ajax.   Thou art indeed a fool,

Thus late i' the day a heart like mine to school.

(*Exeunt.*)

CHORUS.

STROPHE. (*Aria.*)

O famous Salamis, somewhere art thou lying,

Sea-washed and beautiful,

A theme for song for ever ;

And I, unhappy one, these many, many years,

In the pasture-lands of Ida am lingering,

And thro' the long months fretting,

With the miserable expectation

That ere long I shall be journeying

To gloomy Pluto and his dark abode.

ANTISTROPHE.

Now comes, as though we had not enough of trouble,

Ajax, the inflexible,

And the frenzy of heaven's sending.

Him once thou sentest forth in glory to the war ;

D

But now he is become, with his wits a-wandering,

To his friends a shame and sorrow ;

And the great deeds of his arm,

Wrought of old, are all forgotten

By chiefs ungrateful and the host forgotten.

STROPHE.

O ! methinks his aged mother,

His grey-hair'd mother,

When she heareth of his madness,

Will raise a cry,

No musical lament of nightingale,

But a loud and bitter cry,

And with both hands beat her breast,

And tear in agony her poor white hair.

ANTISTROPHE.

Better in his grave, far better,

This madman, Ajax,

Who, coming of the noblest house

Of warlike Greeks,

Shameth his fathers and his former self.

O what a tale to hear,

Father, the sad fate of thy son,

The saddest that thy noble house hath known.

(*Enter* AJAX.)

Time in his long, immeasurable course,

Turns light to darkness, darkness unto light :

Nought is past hoping for : the binding oath

Is found at fault, the stoutest heart gives way.

For I, so stedfast in my firm resolve,

Am softened, like as steel when dipt in oil,

By this poor soul—'twere hard mid foes to leave her,

A widow'd woman with an orphan child.

No—I'll away to the meadows by the shore,

And bathe, and purify myself, and strive

To keep Athene's heavy wrath away.

And, when I come upon some lonely spot,

I will there hide this hated sword of mine,

Deep in the ground where not an eye shall see,

Where Death and Night shall keep it deep below.

For, since the day I took this cursèd gift

From Hector's hands, the Greeks have done me wrong :

Well, well—it seems there's truth i' the old saw,

" Trust not a foe who comes with open hand."

Henceforward, then, we'll bow to Heaven's decrees,

And learn to shew meet reverence to the kings ;

They are our lords ; obedience is their due ;

Yea, things, that hard and most unbending are,

Have sense of order ; so the winter snows

Duly give place to summer fruits and flowers ;

And so the dark and dismal car of Night

Retreats before the white steeds of the Dawn ;

And blasts of stormy winds do raise and lull

The roaring sea, and the mighty hand of Sleep

Binds and lets loose, nor keeps his hold for ever :

Then why not I learn sense ?—of late I've found

A foe is just so far to have your hate,

As one whom chance may prove your friend ere long,

And just so far a friend is to be serv'd,

As who may turn foe o' the morrow—so safe,

Too oft, is friendship's haven to anchor in.

All this, then, shall go well; wherefore, good wife,

Go thou indoors, and pray to the great Gods

To grant fulfilment to my heart's desire;

And you, my friends, pay me that same regard,

And tell to Teucer, when he comes, to shew

His love for me and care withal for you;

Now, do my bidding; maybe, ere long you'll say,

Ajax, tho' beaten, hath yet won the day.

(*Exit.*)

CHORUS.

STROPHE. (*Aria, to quick and lively music.*)

I shudder with delight, and leap for joy;

O Pan, O Pan, come, come across the sea,

Come, thou that leadest the dances of the Gods,

From the snowy ridges of Cyllênê, come,

Join me in the dances free of Nysus and of Knôssus,

For now it is my will to dance.

And thou, Apollo, shining king of Delos,

Let me see thee coming over Icarian waters,

And be my friend, my friend for evermore.

ANTISTROPHE.

Sorrow is gone, our tears are wiped away ;

O Zeus, now shines the bright light of the sun.

Now may we approach our swift-sailing ships,

For our lord hath forgotten all his troubles,

And prayeth to the Gods with holy reverence.

Time, great Time, bringeth all things to nought ;

Nothing shall I call impossible with Time,

Seeing that our lord past our hopes hath chang'd

From his anger and his strife with the brother-kings.

(*Enter* MESSENGER.)

Mess. Friends, my first news is, Teucer is arrived

Fresh from the Mysian heights, but scarce had reach'd

The central camp, before the news had spread

Of his coming, and straight the Argives one and all

To right and left fell on him with abuse ;

" Mad traitor's brother," cried they, as they shower'd

Stones, from the which 'twas well he 'scaped with life.

Swords crossed at length, but when the strife had

                    gone

Its furthest, came the elders and made peace.

But, my lord Ajax—prithee, where is he ?

What news we have 'tis meet my lord should hear.

   Chor. 'Tis but this moment past he went away,

Changed for the better both in word and deed.

   Mess. Alas ! then he who sent me on this errand,

Sent me too late, or I've been long i' the coming.

   Chor. Why, what is wrong ?

   Mess.   Teucer forbad express

Ajax should leave his tent, till he were here.

   Chor. Howe'er that be, the man is gone, and with

The best intent, to make his peace with the Gods.

   Mess. Make peace with the Gods— O these are

                idle words,

If that mean ought which the seer Calchas says.

Chor. Says what? what can he know of matters
    here?

Mess. Thus much I know, for I was there the
    while.

The chiefs were gather'd in a circle round

The brother-kings, when Calchas drew aside,

And grasping Teucer kindly by the hand

Said, "Touching thy brother I most strictly charge thee,

If thou wouldst look upon his face to-morrow,

Keep him this day close prisoner to his tent.

Athênê's wrath," these were the prophet's words,

"Athênê's wrath haunts him this one day more.

For all men of thy brother's burly build,

Whose thews are stronger than their brains, are sure

To incur the sore displeasure of the Gods,

If this their strength breed pride and arrogance.

Now," said the seer, "thy brother scarce had stepp'd

Across his threshold hither, when he prov'd

His folly, for his father wisely bade him

Hope for the victory, but ground his hope

Evermore on the favour of the Gods.

And haughtily and foolishly he replied,

That any coward with God's help might win,

But he would win, whether Heav'n will'd or no.

And once again, when in the tide of fight

Athênê urg'd him on against the foe,

In words of blasphemy he bade her go

And stand by those who needed help, for he

Needed no help of either Gods or man.

With these words he brought down upon his head

The unrelenting anger of the Goddess,

Because, so speaking, he remembered not

With all his might he was but mortal man.

But," said the seer, "if he outlive to-day,

Maybe with Heaven's help we may save him yet."

So spake the prophet, and Teucer straightway rose

And bade me bring this message unto you ;

But if your lord hath slipp'd your hands, so sure

As Calchas is a seer, Ajax is gone.

    Chor.   Tecmessa ! ho Tecmessa !

Hither poor woman, and hear this man, whose words
Stab mortally, I fear, at thy repose.

(*Enter* Tecmessa, *from the tent.*)

Tecm. Why, when I just had gain'd this respite brief
From sorrow, would ye call me forth again?

 Chor. Listen to this man's words ; he brings us
    news
Of Ajax, which it pains my soul to hear.

 Tecm. O me, what sayst thou, man? is there no
    hope?

 Mess. For thee I know not ; but if he be gone,
I fear me there is little hope for him.

 Tecm. Nay, but he is gone ; speak, what dost thou
    mean?

 Mess. 'Twas Teucer's bidding he should keep his
    tent,
And by no means be suffered forth alone.

 Tecm. Where, where is Teucer? and what mean
    these words?

Mess. He is just come, and bids me say, his
       brother
Must keep his tent on peril of his life.

Teem. O miserable me, whence learnt he this?

Mess. Calchas so spake, and on this very day,
This day, so big with fate to him and thee.

Teem. O help me, help me, friends, in my sore need;
Quick, quick; go some, and bring me Teucer here,
Go others to the valleys, east and west,
And track the steps of this unhappy man.
Ah now I see, he spake but to deceive,
And all his ancient love for me is gone.
O, child, what shall I do; I cannot stand:
Nay, nay; I too will go, where'er I can.
Quick, quick, friends—come—we may not tarry now
If we would save him from his own rash hand. (*Exit.*)

Chor. Run, friends; to help the lady in her need
Requires not idle words, but speed, speed, speed.

    (*Exeunt all, by different sides of the stage;
      part of the floor in the after part of the*

*stage is wheeled round, so as to remove the
tent scene, and present a woodland glade;
AJAX alone; his sword fixed with the hilt
in the ground beside him.)*

 Ajax. The sword is standing where 'twill pierce
   the best;
That sword, if one have leisure for the thought,
The gift of Hector, my most hated foe.
Now it stands fix'd in the hostile land of Troy,
New sharpened by the steel-consuming whetstone.
And I have happ'd it carefully all round,
To give a kindly and a speedy death.
So far, all's well; and now, great king of Gods,
Thou first, for so 'tis meet, give me thine aid—
'Tis but a little boon I'll ask of thee—
Send me some herald with the sad report
To Teucer, that his friendly hands be first
To lift me fall'n upon this dripping sword;
For fear some eye unfriendly spy me first,
And cast me forth a prey to the dogs and birds.

This, Zeus, I beg of thee, and pray withal

The herald Hermes of the under-world

To lull me, when the sword hath pierc'd my side,

Swiftly, without a struggle, to my sleep.

And you, ye ever-virgin Powers, I summon,

You, who view all the sorrows of mankind,

Ye venerable, swift Furies, that ye see

How my death comes from the Atreidæ's hand.

O haunt th' accursed wretches to the death,

And as ye see me fall by mine own hand,

So let them fall by the hand they love the best.

Come, O ye swift, avenging Furies, come,

Spare not, but wreak your vengeance on them all.

And thou, O Sun, that climbest the steep sky,

When thou shalt look upon my father-land,

There stay thy golden reins, and tell the tale

Of my sorrows and my death to my old father

And my poor mother—ah me ! alas poor mother,

What cries will thine be, when thou hear'st the tale.

But truce to sorrow—to work—and quickly too :

O Death, O Death, come now and gaze upon me—

And yet I soon shall see thee face to face.

And, O thou bright light of the shining day,

And thou, careering Sun, I call upon you,

For the last, last time, and never more again.

O light, O sacred soil of my native earth,

Mine own isle Salamis, and my father's home,

Ye founts and rivers, and ye plains of Troy,

I call upon you—fare ye well, old friends—

These words speaks Ajax with his latest breath ;

All else i' the realms below he'll speak with Death.

> (*Falls upon his sword; as he falls forward,*
>
> *the Semi-Chorus, rushing in from one side,*
>
> *hide him from the audience, and occupy*
>
> *half the front part of the stage.*)

Chor. 1. Labour, labour, labour all in vain !

Whither, whither, O whither have I not been ?

But not one spot can tell me where he is—

But hist ! methinks I hear a sound—who's there ?

> (*Enter the other Semi-Chorus from the other side.*)

Chor. 2. Messmates and friends.

Chor. 1.   What tidings do ye bring ?

Chor. 2. We scour'd the land to westward of the
                fleet.

Chor. 1. And found ?

Chor. 2.   Found nothing, tho' we lost our breath.

Chor. 1. We too have traversed all the eastern side,
But not a sign or trace was to be seen.

CHORUS (*Aria*).

Come, fisher, from thy wakeful toil,
    Come, Nymph, or River-god,
Come, guide our wand'ring steps, and shew
    The path our Ajax trod.
O after roaming on the seas,
    And watching on the plain,
Sore task it is for weary limbs
    To toil, and toil in vain.

Tecm. O, O, O me ! (*from the after part of the
        stage.*)

Chor. Whose voice is this, comes from the grove
      hard by?

Tecm. Me miserable! me miserable!

Chor. I see the captive lady of our lord,
Tecmessa, quite heart-broken with her sorrow.

Tecm. O friends, my life is gone, clean gone for ever.

Chor. What is it, lady?

Tecm.   See, my lord lies here,
The sword within his breast, and newly dead.

Chor. Alas, alas, no chance of home again!
When thou didst fall, we all fell down with thee,
Thy comrades all, and this poor lady here.

Tecm. Ah me! we've food enough for sorrow here.

Chor. Poor man! whose hand was it that dealt
      the blow?

Tecm. His own—See here, his sword is tight i' the
      ground,
And he has flung himself upon the point.

Chor. That such a man should come to such an end!
And not one friend beside him! fool that I was,

Fool, fool to let him go—where does he lie

Our headstrong, our unlucky-named Aias?

(Moving towards the after part of the stage.)

Tecm. (beckoning them back). Not to be look'd

upon—from head to foot

In this his cloak I wrap him round, for sure

No one, that is a friend, would have the heart

To see the black blood bubbling from his mouth,

And the broad gash, self sought, upon his breast.

What shall I do? what friend will bear thee off?

O Teucer, come; thou art sore needed here:

Come, Teucer, come and close thy brother's eyes.

Ah! my poor Ajax, is it come to this?

A sight to melt an enemy to tears.

CHORUS (*Aria*).

The mutter'd words by night and day,

The gloom, the knitted brow,

We knew not what they meant: alas,

'Tis clear as noon-day now.

E

O, Ajax, 'twas a fatal day

    When on the ground were thrown

The chieftain's arms ; that day began

    Thy sorrows and our own.

Teem. O me ; O me !

Chor. True grief, I know, doth pierce to the very

    heart.

Teem. O me ; O me !

Chor. For such sad words thou hast too good a

    cause ;

Thou, who hast lost so lately such a friend.

Teem. So thinkest thou ; so to my cost know I.

We are slaves, my child ; we are no longer free ;

Stern masters and hard work await us now.

Chor. Stern tho' our chieftains be, they are not yet

So hard of heart as to press farther on

Your misery : no, no ; may the Gods forbid !

Teem. They might as easily have forbidden this.

Chor. They have indeed press'd heavily upon

    you.

Tecm. 'Tis all the terrible Athênê's doing,
All for her favourite of Ithaca.

Chor. The much-enduring man, th' inscrutable,
He must have laugh'd indeed, and with him laugh'd
The brother-kings of Sparta and Mycône.

Tecm. Ah, let them laugh and revel in his woes!
Maybe, for all they slighted him in life,
The day will come, when, in the press of war,
They'll miss his arm and wish him back again.
More bitter unto me than sweet to them
Is this his death: but still 'twas his own pleasure:
Then on what grounds should these men laugh at him?
'Twas of heaven's doing that he died, not theirs;
Then let Ulysses have his silly laugh:
Ajax they have no longer;—but to me
Sorrow is left, sorrow for evermore.

        (A cry is heard from behind the scenes.)

  Chor. Hush, hush: 'tis Teucer's voice, and from
            the sound
'Twould seem he knew what sorrow waits him here.

(*Enter* Teucer.)

Teu. O Ajax, Ajax ! O my own dear brother!
And has it fared with thee as rumour tells ?

Chor. Teucer, 'tis all too true—Ajax is dead.

Teu. O wretched me—this is too hard to bear.

Chor. There is indeed too good a cause for tears.

Teu. O wretched me !   O loss most terrible !

Chor. Too terrible, indeed.

Teu.   Where is his child ?
Where in the Troad is the little one ?

Chor. Alone within the tent.

Teu.   Go, with all speed :
The lioness is left alone, and foes
Will seize upon the cub that's left behind—
Haste, haste—too many will make haste to tread
Upon his back, whose face is to the ground.

Chor. Teucer, this zeal in the poor child's behalf,
Is but the purport of his last command.

Teu. O, of all sights most terrible to me,
The saddest that these eyes e'er look'd upon ;

And of all journeys I e'er undertook,

Most melancholy this, whereon I learnt

That thou wast dead, dear Ajax, dead and gone.

For swifter far than human tongue could bear,

Thro' all the host the fatal news had spread ;

And the mere hearing made me sad enough,

But now the sight itself will drive me mad.

O me !

Come, let me lift this cloak, and see it all—

Poor face, what stern resolve its look bespeaks :

This deed of thine leaves me a load of sorrow—

Where can I shew my forehead ? I that left thee

To struggle with thy misery all alone—

Methinks our father Telamon, when I come

Without thee, with a kind and welcome face

Will greet me—he, a man, whose countenance

Was of the grimmest in his best of moods.

What words upon my head will he forbear

To heap ? " The foreign woman's base-born brat,

That left his brother in his hour of need,

From cowardice or treacherous intent,

To hold the place and honours of the dead;"

So will the old man speak, fretful with age,

And quick to quarrel at a word or look;

And he will turn me out of doors at last,

An exile, branded with the name of slave.

So much for my home welcome; and in Troy

My foes are many, and my friends are few:

And all this misery cometh by thy death.

Ah me! what shall I do? how can I pluck

Out of thy body the sharp, gleaming steel,

That let thy life out!—See'st thou, how at length

Hector was doom'd e'en dead to work thine end?

I pray you note the fate of these two men;

'Twas by the girdle Ajax gave to him

That Hector to the chariot-rim was tied

And dragg'd along, until he breathed his last;

And, see, the sword, on which this man hath fall'n,

Was Hector's gift to him: methinks, the sword

Was of some Fury's forging, and the belt

The work of Death, a craftsman terrible :—

For mine own part, in these things and the like

I evermore shall see the hand of Gods

Dealing with man ; who thinketh otherwise,

May keep his own thoughts, and let me keep mine.

    Chor. Cut short thy words, and think how we shall lay

               shall lay

This man in his grave ; and, if one question thee,

Be ready with an answer, for I see

An enemy coming, and he comes, methinks,

To scoff, the villain, at our misery.

    Teu. Who comes ?

    Chor.   The prince of Sparta, Menelaus,

Whose troubles brought us hither.

    Teu.   Ay, I see ;

At this short distance it were hard to miss.

        (*Enter* MENELAUS.)

    Mene. Ho, sirrah, see thou venture not to raise

That body from the ground : let it lie there.

Teu. And, prithee, wherefore all this waste of words?

Mene. I speak mine own will and the will of him,

Who is the lord and captain of the host.

Teu. And may we hear the cause of this same will?

Mene. The cause is simple: we had thought to bring

This man from home an ally and a friend,

And he was found upon experiment

More dangerous than any open foe:

The wretch, who schem'd the murder of us all,

And under cover of the night set forth

To put his bloody purpose to effect;

And, but that heaven had quenched the mad attempt,

A fate were ours ignoble as his own,

And he were living now; but the Gods turn'd

His ruthless hand against the flocks and herds.

No man is, then, so strong, as who shall dare

To lay him in his grave in my despite,

But sea-birds first shall have their feast, and leave

Upon the yellow sand his mouldering bones.

Wherefore restrain thy temper and thy tongue;

For, tho' the man gave us scant heed in life,

We'll lord it o'er him dead, say what thou wilt,

And mould him to our will; for, sooth to say,

That will was little heeded heretofore.

And yet 'tis most unseemly that a man,

One of the many, should refuse to pay

Obedience to his betters ; for in a state

No laws could have their due effect, unless

The sense of fear were in a people's heart ;

Nor could an army be well led, that lack'd

The sense of order and respect of place.

A man should reckon, be he ne'er so big,

The smallest pebble may trip up his heels.

But, where obedience and respect is found,

There is found safety ; but in man or state,

Where wilfulness and outrage rule the day,

That state or man will drive before the wind

Sooner or later on a shore of ruin.

Nay, nay ; let us shew fear where fear is due,

Remembering evermore that, if we shape

Our actions to our pleasure, other hands

May shape their consequences to our pain.

There is a see-saw in these things ; for once

'Twas this man's turn to bluster, now 'tis mine.

Wherefore I pray thee, busy not thyself

With this man's burial, lest, as thou shalt bend

Over his grave, thou topple into thine own.

    Chor. Prince, when thou can'st propound such
                  weighty rules

Of conduct, it becomes thee ill to mar

Their good effect by outrage to the dead.

    Teu. I shall not be disposed to wonder, friends,

To see some base-born fellow play the fool,

When men, reputed of most ancient birth,

Display such arrant folly in their words—

Tell me, Sir Prince, came Ajax at the first

An ally of thy bringing to the war?

Was not the fleet, he sailed withal, his own?

Was he not master of himself? Then how

Art thou his lord? how art thou king of men,

That under Ajax came from Salamis ?

Thou 'rt lord of Sparta, and no king of ours :

To order this man's goings thou hast no more

Of right, than he would have to order thine :

Thou camest under others ; not supreme,

That Ajax should owe fealty to thee.

Go rule where thou hast right to rule, and vent

Thy pride ; but for the man who lieth here,

Say thou and say thy brother what ye will,

I tell ye both, I 'll lay him in his grave,

As a prince should be laid, for all your threats.

'T was not thy wife that brought him to the war,

The sorry cause that brought the plodding herd ;

It was the oath that bound him, and no cause

Of thine, for he set little store on fools.

Go, fetch a crowd of servants, and my lord,

The general ; as for me, I will not stir

One inch, whilst thou art what I take thee for.

    Chor. And thy words too are out of time ; such words

How just so e'er they be, cut to the quick.

Mene. The archer seems contented with himself.

Teu. The archer's trade may justify content.

Mene. How he would bluster if he wore a sword.

Teu. My bow were match for any sword of thine.

Mene. Thy spirit must be high indeed, if we
May judge it by thy tongue.

Teu.   High words
Are all in place, with justice on their side.

Mene. Justice! and seems it just this man should go
Unpunished, after he has murdered me.

Teu. Murder'd thee! heav'ns, what can the fellow
                        mean?
He must be living-dead or dead-alive.

Mene. That I am now alive, the Gods be thank'd;
It were not so, had this man had his way.

Teu. Slight not the Gods, if they have been so
                        kind.

Mene. And wherein, prithee, do I slight the Gods?

Teu. By staying thus the burial of the dead.

Mene. He was mine enemy: I am in my right.

Teu. Why, how was Ajax enemy of thine ?

Mene. Our hate was mutual, as thou know'st right
     well.

Teu. Ay, ay ; the votes had foul play at thy
     hands.

Mene. The loss, thou hintest at, was the award
Of the judges and not me.

Teu.   Ay, thou can'st do
Mischief enough, and do it in the dark.

Mene. Thou shalt most bitterly rue this insolence.

Teu. Whate'er I get, I will give back in kind.

Mene. These few words more ; "Thou shalt not
     bury him."

Teu. And I will answer thee in two ; "I will."

Mene. Once on a time I saw a braggart knave,
The while a storm was brewing, urging on
His messmates to set sail ; but, when
The storm was fairly on, the man was dumb,
And underneath his cloak lay on the deck,
A mat for all that chose to trample on—

And so with thee and with thy blust'ring tongue,

Maybe a flood out from some little cloud

Will burst, and lay this windy storm of words.

    Teu. I, too, once saw a man with folly brimm'd,

Whose chief delight was in his neighbour's woes ;

And there stood by him one like me in face

And temper, and on this wise counsell'd him ;

" Good friend be not unfeeling towards the dead,

Else others prove unfeeling towards thee :"

Such was the counsel given the graceless man—

And now, if these eyes cheat me not, I see

The man before me—Is my riddle plain ?

    Mene. I will begone : it is poor chastisement

To use harsh words, when one may use harsh means.

    Teu. Ay, get thee gone ; I am ashamed thus long

To listen to the folly of a fool.

               (*Exit* MENELAUS.)

    Chor. (*advancing*). Mischief will come of this ; so

              with all speed

Search, Teucer, for some spot where we may dig

A hollow grave, which, famous among men,

Shall be the hero's earthly resting-place.

(*Enter* TECMESSA *and child.*)

Teu. See, friends, as though their footsteps had

been timed

To suit our wishes, come his wife and child,

To pay the last sad honours to the dead.

Come hither, child, and sit thee down beside

Thy father, with one hand upon his breast,

And in the other hold these locks of hair,

Thy mother's, mine and thine ; then, if one dare

To tear thee rudely from the dead man's side,

My curse be on him ; may his life be spent

In exile ; may his body be cast forth

Unsepultur'd; and, as this lock I sever,

So perish he, his kindred, root and branch.

Here, child, take this and guard it well ; let none

Remove thee, but kneel down and keep fast hold.

And you, my friends, be men, and shield from harm

These twain till I return, which will not be

Till all be ready, let who will say Nay.

(*Exit* Teucer.)

CHORUS.

STROPHE (*Aria*).

Wearily roll the long years by ;

    Comes pause to sorrow never ;

Old troubles end, new troubles rise,

    As they would last for ever :

Beneath Troy's walls, on her broad plain

We have bled freely and in vain.

ANTISTROPHE.

My curse upon the scheming knave,

    Who set our chiefs in motion ;

He should have died, before a sail

    Were set across the Ocean ;

Then many a man were safe and sound,

That now lies sleeping under ground.

STROPHE.

No dances cheer the lagging hours,
    No sound of music now ;
No brimming wine-cup fills my hand,
    No wreath entwines my brow.
And love is a forgotten theme ;
    Forgotten is all joy :
Our days are full of fears, our nights
    Chill'd with the dews of Troy.

ANTISTROPHE.

And this our safeguard in the dark,
    Our buckler thro' the day,
Is gone ; and with his parting breath
    Our hopes are fled away.
O would we were safe round the cape,
    That frowns upon the sea,
With Athens on our starboard-bow,
    And home upon our lee.

F

(*Enter* AGAMEMNON.)

   Agam. They tell me, sir, that thou hast dar'd to
        speak
In rebel terms of my authority,
Regardless of the pains such words incur ;
That thou hast dar'd, the captive woman's son :
Heav'ns, if thy mother had been of gentle birth,
Thy pride would walk on tip-toe, and thy tongue
Would freely wag, if base-born thou presum'st
To champion one no better than thyself.
So we are come, say'st thou, without command
Of Grecian fleets or Grecian soldiery ;
And Ajax owed obedience to none :
This is indeed high language for a slave.
Who was this man, of whom these vaunts are made ?
Where'er he went or stood, was I not found ?
Was he of all Achæans the one man ?
Methinks we have good reason to repent
The contest for the arms, if Teucer here

Be free on all occasions to impugn

The justice of our motives ; and if you

Cry out against a sentence duly giv'n ;

If we must be expos'd to ribald words

From you, and treachery, you beaten men.

If things go thus, no law can have effect ;

If, when one wins his cause, we set aside

His rights, and push the hindmost to the front.

This must not be ; 'tis not your brawny men

That are the safest in the hour of need ;

Wisdom in one and all things bears the palm.

Your ox, for all its ponderous flanks, a child

May drive before him with a little goad—

And now, methinks, unless thou take good heed,

Some such appliance must be used with thee.

The man is dead and gone, in whose behalf

Thou givest such license to thy flippant tongue.

Learn sense : consider who and what thou art,

And go, and fetch me, sir, some one free-born,

Who may interpret what thou hast to say,

For words of thine were thrown away on me ;
I have such poor skill in these foreign tongues.

    Chor. I pray you curb these tempers ; it may be
Poor counsel, sirs, but 'tis the best I have.

    Teu. Alas ! when once a man is dead, how soon
The memory of his good deeds fades away,
When this man, Ajax, for whose sake thy life
Was perill'd many a time, begrudges thee
The sorry tribute of one kindly word :
Nay, all is gone, clean gone, and quite forgotten—
Thou foolish man, dost thou remember not,
When ye were in the toils, when hope was gone,
How in the turn of fight this man alone
Sav'd you, when now the ships were in a blaze,
And down among you all great Hector came,
Taking the trenches at a flying bound ?
Who saved you then ? was it not this man here ?
Did this man so, or am I speaking lies ?
Again, when lots were cast, he freely took
The issue, and met Hector face to face :

The lot he cast into the helmet then

Was not your coward's bit of crumbling earth,

But such a pebble, round and smooth, as might

Leap out at the first rattling of the brass :

This was the man, and by his side stood I,

The foreigner, the slave, the captive's son.

Wretch ! dar'st thou look me in the eyes, and speak

These words, when thou the while must know right well

Pelops, the founder of thy line, to be.

No Hellên, but a Phrygian foreigner ?

Thy father, Atreus, was the guilty wretch,

Who banqueted a brother on the flesh

Of that same brother's children ; and thy mother

Was Cretan-born, and she, surpris'd one day

With her paramour, was hurl'd into the sea

To feed the silent fishes—and dost thou

With such a lineage dare to carp at mine ?

My sire was Telamon, the foremost man

Of Grecian warriors, and he took to wife

My mother, princess of a royal house,

Child of Laomedon, whom Alcmene's son

Gave to my father as a prize of war.

Shall I then, sprung from this most noble pair,

See outrage done to mine own flesh and blood,

My brother, whom in this extremity

Thou wouldst cast forth, nor blush to give the word ?

Learn this, wherever thou shalt cast him forth,

There shalt thou cast his wife and child and me.

For unto me it were more honourable

To die before the world in his behalf,

Than fighting for thine own or brother's wife :

Wherefore, look well unto thyself, not me ;

For, if thou dost me harm, may be one day

Thou'lt wish thy valour had been dash'd with fear.

(*Enter* ULYSSES.)

Chor. My lord Ulysses, thou art come in time,

If thou art come to part these disputants.

Ulys. What is it friends ? for from afar I heard

The General's voice over this valiant dead.

Agam. No wonder, for but now we were assail'd
By this man here with the most vile abuse.

Ulys. How so ?   I can well feel for any man
That giveth like for like.

Agam.   'Twas so with me ;
His acts began it, and I paid in words.

Ulys. What had he done this anger to incur ?

Agam. He swears this body shall not be deprived
The rites of burial, and that his own hands
Will lay it in the grave in my despite.

Ulys. May then a friend speak out the honest truth,
Nor forfeit friendship ?

Agam.   Speak ; it were unwise
To take amiss the words of my best friend.

Ulys. Hear then——I do adjure thee by the Gods,
Cast not this body forth thus ruthlessly ;
And let not passion master thee so far,
That thou should'st tread on right to glut thy hate.
For I too had in him my bitterest foe
After the contest for the arms ; but still

Remembering who he was, I cannot force

My conscience to deny this testimony,

That, save Achilles, he was of us all

The bravest soldier that set sail for Troy.

Thou hast no right then to dishonour him ;

For not to him, but to the Gods below

The wrong were done ; and most unjust it were,

Be hatred ne'er so strong, to harm a man,

A worthy man, when dead and on the ground.

    Agam. Speaking these words, Ulysses, thou dost

                plead

His cause against thy friend.

    Ulys.   I do indeed ;

And yet he had my hate, while hate was fair.

    Agam. Is it so wrong to trample on the dead ?

    Ulys. It were a triumph a good man would spurn.

    Agam. It is not easy for a king to weigh

Right in so nice a balance.

    Ulys.   But a king

Can lend an ear to a true friend's advice.

Agam. One who is loyal to a king should learn
Obedience.

Ulys. Nay, my lord, press not so far
Thy resolution ; whoso to a friend
Submits, is of the twain the conqueror.

Agam. Bethink thee what this fellow was, to
whom
Thou shew'st such kindness.

Ulys. I remember well ;
He was my foe, but a good man withal.

Agam. What? would'st respect the body of a foe !

Ulys. Yea, for his worth is stronger than my
hate.

Agam. Methinks, such words do savour of a heart
Too shallow to conceive or love or hate.

Ulys. Sometimes the man who went to sleep your
friend,
Wakes up an enemy.

Agam. And would'st thou advise
Winning such friendship.

Ulys.   I would advise, my lord,
A firm resolve, but not obduracy.

Agam. Thou'lt make us cowards in the eyes of all.

Ulys. Not cowards ; nay, but honourable men.

Agam. Thou'dst have me grant, then, burial to
          this dead ?

Ulys. I would, my lord ; for I must go one day,
Where Ajax is already.

Agam.   Even so ;
In every action is the trace of self.

Ulys. Myself seems the best motive for myself.

Agam. Well, well; take thou the deed upon
          thyself.

Ulys. Howe'er 'tis done, the credit rests with thee.

Agam. I yield me then, but I must state withal,
That, tho' I would do more than this for thee,
Yet this man, as in life, so here in death,
I hated and shall hate him to the last—
And now do with him what it pleaseth thee.

                              (*Exit.*)

Chor. Whoso, Ulysses, after deeds like this,

Denies thee wisdom, is himself a fool.

Ulys. And, Teucer, now I proffer thee my hand,

A sworn foe hitherto, henceforth a friend ;

And let me bear a hand in these sad rites,

And shew, as all we mortal men are bound

To shew, my honour for a brave, good man.

Teu. Ulysses, I do thank thee from my heart ;

Thou hast most honourably belied my hopes,

For thou, albeit this man's most bitter foe,

Alone hast helped us in our need, alone

Hast scorn'd' to mock the unresisting dead ;

Not like yon pair of thunder-stricken fools,

Who came to insult this body, and to cast

It forth without the honour of a grave.

For this I do beseech the Olympian sire,

The wakeful Furies and the dreaded Power

Of Retribution, that their end may be

In keeping with their wishes to the dead.

But thou, Ulysses, old Laertes' son,

In this one thing I cannot take thine aid,

For fear I do displeasure to the dead :

But give thy help some other form, or bring

Some other of the chiefs to take thy place.

Now to my business ; I will add but this,

Thou'st proved thyself to us a friend indeed.

    Ulys. I could have wish'd it otherwise, but since

It is thy will, I yield and say Farewell.

(Exit.)

    Teu. 'Tis good : we've wasted time enough : so

        come,

Dig some of you a hollow trench ; and some

Prepare the lustral waters ; others go,

And fetch the hero's armour from the tent.

And thou, child, with what little strength thou hast,

Clasp tenderly with me thy father's form,

And lift it gently—-very gently, child,

For the black blood still swells i' the warm veins.

And hasten all of you ; do what ye can

Of service for a man as good and true,

As you or I shall live to see again.

       (Exit slowly, carrying the body of AJAX.*)*

Chor. (*retiring slowly.*) To see is to believe ; but,

       till we see,

To-morrow's life is veil'd to you and me.

       (Exeunt to a funeral march.)

IPHIGENIA IN AULIS.

Observations.—CALCHAS has notified that the hopes of the whole expedition to Troy depend on the sacrifice of IPHIGENIA. AGAMEMNON, as instructed by a council of elders, sends a letter to CLYTEMNESTRA, requesting her to bring her daughter to the camp to be married to ACHILLES. At the last moment his courage fails him, and in a second letter he tells her the whole plot, and begs her to devise some excuse for not coming. This letter is intercepted by MENELAUS. The mother and daughter arrive at the camp; the following scene opens just after they have learned privately the real object of their coming.

IPHIGENIA IN AULIS.

——◆——

Aulis; the camp, in front of AGAMEMNON's *tent. Enter*
CLYTEMNESTRA *from the tent.*

Clyt. Where is this Agamemnon ? I would fain
Behold this father, who is soon to dye
His hands unnatural in a daughter's blood.

(*Enter* AGAMEMNON *from the side.*)

Agam. Daughter of Leda, very seasonably
I find thee here, for I would speak with thee
Alone, of matters which it were unfit
Our child, the bride-elect, should overhear.

Clyt. And to what purpose is the moment tim'd ?

Agam. The lustral-waters are prepar'd ; the meal
To scatter on the purifying flame ;

The kids, that ere the bridal-day must fall

To Artemis, the sacrifice of blood ;

So tell the child her father waits her here.

    Clyt.   These are fair words ; (*aside*) methinks,

             'twere hard to find

Words that would shew their hidden purport fair.

        (*Retreats towards the tent-door, and holding it*

           open, speaks in an under-tone to IPHIGENIA

           within.)

Come hither, child ; thou know'st thy father's wish ;

And bring with thee, under thy mantle's fold,

Thy little brother Orestes.

    (*re-advancing*)   See, my lord,

Here is thy child, obedient to thy will :

Let me be speaker now for her and me.

    Agam.   Why weep, my child ? and wherefore meet

           me not

With the old smile ? why is thy face cast down ?

And wherefore with thy mantle shade thine eyes ?

    Clyt. Alas ! alas !

Which of my griefs shall first find utterance?

All are so great, that they will all come first,

And none will yield to other precedence.

Agam. What meaneth this? why, ye are all alike,

And trouble's writ on every countenance.

Clyt. I'll put a question to thee, and do thou

Give me an answer honest and direct.

    Agam. That needs no bidding: speak; I am all

        ears.

    Clyt. Thy daughter, thine and mine — dost mean

        to kill her?

Agam. Ah!

Why, that were monstrous; surely in thy brain

Suspicions lurk, that have no business there.

    Clyt. That matters not; answer my question first.

    Agam. Merciful heavens! what a fate is mine!

    Clyt. And mine, and hers; a sad one for all three.

    Agam. What harm's been done?

    Clyt.   What? Askest that of me?—

The plan is deep; but one may fathom it.

G

Agam.   I am undone : my secret is betray'd.

Clyt.   Ay, 'tis no secret ; we have heard it all.

There is no need to rack thy brain for words ;

Thy silence and thy sighs speak plain enough.

Agam.   I have no answer ; none : my grief so

      great

Needs not the base addition of a lie.

Clyt.   Listen then ; listen ; I will now speak plain,

And drop this speech of hint and parable.

First then, to let my angry words maintain

Due time and sequence, I was at the first

Made wife of thine by durance and constraint ;

My husband, Tantalus, was slain by thee ;

By thee my baby from my breast was torn,

Torn by those pitiless hands, and dashed to earth.

My brothers twain, the hero-sons of Zeus,

Mounted their shining cars in hot pursuit ;

Thou fled'st a suppliant to my father's feet ;

He rais'd thee ; pardon'd thee, and gave thee life,

Thy forfeited life, and his own daughter's hand.

And I forgave thee all, and thou wilt own

That I was blameless towards thee and thine,

A chaste and virtuous wife, that order'd well

Thy house, so that thou wert a happy man

In all thy goings out and comings in.

And such a wife is not found by the way;

Your thriftless ones are plentiful as weeds.

Three children bare I unto thee, whereof

This boy is youngest-born; and of the three

Thou hast the heart to rob me of this girl.

If one should ask thee, "Wherefore dost thou kill her?"

What wouldst thou answer?—shall I answer for thee?

"That Menelaus may win Helen back."

Heav'ns! 'tis a grand exchange for us to give

Our children, to redeem a worthless jade:

With what we love we purchase what we hate.

Come, if thou leavest me at home, to pass

Thyself long years out yonder in the war,

What, thinkest thou, will be my thoughts at home,

When I shall see my daughter's vacant place,

And vacant chamber, when alone I brood

Over my sorrows, making ceaseless moan,

" My child, my child, thy father slew thee, child,

Thy father his own child, with his own hand."

    Tempt me not, I beseech thee by the Gods,

To be thine enemy, and be not thou

Thine own worst enemy—little would suffice

For me and for the children left behind,

To make us render thee on thy return

The welcome thou deservest at our hands.

        (*A long pause, during which she gazes fixedly*

           on AGAMEMNON, *who stands silent and*

           motionless.)

Well ; be it so ; and thou wilt slay the child :

And, prithee, what will be thy words of prayer,

And what will be the blessing thou call'st down

Upon thine own head, as thou killest her ?

Or were it right that I should pray for thee ?

Methinks it were an insult to the Gods

To ask their blessing on a murderer.

And when thou comest home, wilt thou embrace
Thy children? nay, thou wilt have lost all right;
And which of them will dare present itself
Before thee, to be made a sacrifice?

Is all thine office circumscrib'd to this,
To wield a sceptre and to marshal men?
Why speak not words of reason to the host;
" Achæans, would ye sail to Phrygian land?
Then cast the lots, whose daughter is to die."
For this were fair, and not that thou shouldst be
Thus singled out to sacrifice thy child;
Or that thy brother, whom it most concerns,
Should give Hermione in her mother's stead.
No; I, that have been true to thee, must lose
My child, and the wanton find on her return
A living daughter and a happy home.

Tell me, if any of my words be wrong;
If they be right—O, I intreat thee, spare
Our child, and thou wilt be a wise, good man.

    Iphig.   O, if I had the voice of Orpheus, father,

To draw the stones with music after me,

And charm with words each listener to my will,

I would use words ; now use I what I have,

My tears ; I have nought else to plead for me.

I am thy child, born to thee of this lady,

And I entreat thee, clinging to thy knees,

Slay me not in the spring-tide of my days ;

Life is so sweet, so sweet ; O force me not

Out of my happy youth into my grave.

I am thy first-born ; it was my voice first

That babbled "father ;" first upon thy knee

'Twas I that sat, caressing and caress'd.

And thou wouldst often say, " I wonder, child,

If I shall see thee grown to womanhood,

And in some prince's house a happy wife,

In state, as suits the daughter of a king."

And, playing with thy beard, which now I hold

A humble suppliant, I would make reply ;

" I wonder if the days will ever come,

When thou shalt have grown old, and I shall have

A home wherein to welcome thee and pay

Thy former love by nursing thy grey hairs."

All this I do remember well, but thou

Forgettest, and thou seekest my young life.

O by the shades of our great ancestors,

Have mercy on me, and for my mother's sake,

Who at my death will feel a second time

The pangs she suffer'd when she gave me birth.—

Why, what had I to do with Helen's loves?

And how should Paris come to ruin me?

Nay, father, look on me, give me one kiss,

And, if thou wilt not hearken to my prayer,

And I must die, then I will take the kiss

Away with me in memory of thy love.

And thou, my brother, little as thou art,

Do what thou canst, and join thy tears with mine,

And of thy father beg thy sister's life;

Even thy little brain may dimly guess

What sorrow means—see! without words he prays;

Two, whom thou lovest, are clinging to thy knees;

Thine infant boy, thy daughter in her prime.

But one word more ; to all men life is sweet,

And death's a blank ; who prays to die is mad ;

Better is shame in life than glory in one's grave.

 Agam. I am not steel'd to pity ; I do love

My children ; I were mad, an 'twere not so.

Lady, I have strong reason for the deed,

Strong reason to refrain : there is no help.

Look round, and see this fleet of serried ships ;

These chieftains, leaders all of armed men ;—

These men, so Calchas the old seer proclaims,

May never spread a sail across the sea,

May never take the far-famed walls of Troy,

If I refuse to offer thee my child.

And all the host is smitten with a wild

And passionate longing to set sail forthwith,

And they will rise and slay us one and all,

Here and in Argos, if I disobey.

I am not slave to Menelaus, child,

Nor are my doings fram'd to humour him ;

No, 'tis for Hellas I must offer thee,

Our fatherland : to her we must give way :

And thou and I, child, must do all we can

To keep her free, nor let these foreigners come

And stain the honour of Hellenic wives.

(Exit Agamemnon.)

THE SHIELD OF ACHILLES.

——◆——

And first he made a buckler, great and strong,

All over chasing it, and round it threw

A shining rim, triple-fold, glittering,

And made a belt of silver ; and there were

Five folds unto the shield, and on the front

Devices strange of subtlest workmanship.

    Therein he plac'd the earth, the heaven, the sea,

The Sun unwearied and the full-faced Moon,

And all the stars wherewith the sky is crowned,

The Pleiads, Hyads, and Orion's might,

And Arctus, called by mortal men the Wain,

That dogs Orion, turning on one spot,

Alone unwashed by old Oceanus.

And therein placed he cities twain of men,
Beautiful ; bridals there and banquetings ;
And from their chambers thro' a city's streets
By torchlight they were leading brides, and loud
The marriage-hymn was rising, and the youths
Were whirling in the dance, and in the midst
The flutes and lyres were sounding, and good wives
Were standing at their doors in wonderment.

And in the market-place a crowd of men
Was gathered, for a quarrel had arisen :
There strove two men about the price of blood
Of a slain man ; and of the twain one sware
The price was paid, the other still said, Nay.
And both made haste to bring their cause before
An umpire ; and the crowd were of two minds,
With this man siding some, and some with that.
And there were heralds keeping back the crowd,
And in a sacred circle on smooth stones
The elders were there seated, staff in hand ;
And with the staves they turn'd to right and left,

Hearing both sides; and in the midst there lay

Two talents weight of gold, to give to him

Whoso should seem to plead his cause aright.

    And round the second city were encamped

Two hosts of people, glittering in arms,

Whose counsel was divided; some were fain

To storm the city and divide the spoil,

All that the goodly city held within;

Others were bent upon an ambuscade:

But on the city's walls there stood on guard

Women and little lads and aged men;

So the others started, and before them went

Pallas Athênê, and the God of war,

Both wrought in gold, with golden garments clad,

Both beautiful and tall, as Gods should be,

In armour, and distinct from all the rest,

For those they led were puny in compare.

And when they reached the place of ambuscade

By a river's side where cattle came to drink,

There sat they down, all clad in shining mail:

And at a distance from them sat two spies,

To wait the coming of the flocks and herds ;

And these came soon, and herdsmen twain behind

Playing their pipes, without a thought of guile ;

And they in ambush, seeing them, rush'd forth,

And straightway slew the herds and goodly flocks

Of white-fleeced sheep, and slew the herdsmen too.

And the others, seated in the agora,

Hearing the din and lowing of the herds,

Mounted their cars, and to the rescue came ;

And there they stood, and by the river's side

Joined fight ; and spears and arrows flew apace.

And Strife and Tumult mingled in the fray,

And dreaded Doom, holding one man alive

Just wounded, and another without hurt,

One she was dragging by both feet, stone-dead ;

And all her garments were dyed red with blood.

And they, like mortal men, joined in the fight,

And dragg'd the corses from each other's hands.

And therein placed he a soft fallow-land,

A corn-field rich, and broad and triple-plough'd ;

And in the corn-field many husbandmen

Were driving teams of oxen to and fro ;

And when they reach'd the limits of the field,

One coming forward plac'd a cup of wine

Into their hands ; and they turn'd back in haste

To reach the limits of the field again.

And all the ground was black, as ground when plough'd,

Tho' wrought in gold : so wondrous was the work.

    And therein placed he a rich field of corn,

And reapers with sharp sickles in their hands

Were reaping ; and some handfuls to the ground

Along the furrow in a line were falling,

Others the binders fastened into sheaves

(For there were three sheaf-binders), and behind

The lads were busy gleaning their laps full :

Among them, staff in hand, the Farmer stood,

In silence on the furrow, glad at heart.

And serving-men far off beneath an oak

Prepar'd a feast, for they had slain an ox,

And therewithal were busy ; and the while

The women-folk were sprinkling a good store

Of barley for the reapers' evening meal.

  And therein likewise he a vineyard plac'd,

Heavy with bunches, beautiful, in gold ;

And purple were the clusters ; and it stood

With props of silver piercèd thro' and thro'.

A dark-blue trench and hedge went round about

Of tin ; and hereunto one pathway led,

Whereby the men at vintage came and went.

And lads and lasses in the bloom of youth

Were gathering in baskets the rich fruit ;

And in the midst upon a full-ton'd lyre

A lad was sweetly playing, and to the lyre

Was singing an ancient ditty with clear voice ;

And to the music they were keeping time

With song and cries and movements of the limbs.

  And therein was a herd of horned kine,

That were all wrought of mingled gold and tin ;

They lowing from their stalls to pasture went,

To a sounding stream, swift-flowing, thick with reeds.

And herdsmen, wrought in gold, went with the herds.

Four, and nine dogs swift-footed came behind ;

And two fierce lions in the front had hold

Both of one bull, who loudly bellowing

Was being dragg'd along, and youths and hounds

Were following in pursuit, and the lions twain

Were lapping up the entrails and black blood ;

And the youths stood frighten'd, and cheer'd on the
      hounds ;

But the hounds refrain'd from closing with the beasts,

But stood and bark'd, and still kept out of reach.

   And therein the illustrious Lame-God wrought

A pasture full of sheep, in a rich vale,

With stalls and pens and shelter'd, close-roof'd sheds.

   A choral dance he also placed therein,

Like to that one, which in wide Knôssus once

Dædalus for fair-hair'd Ariadne wrought.

And therein youths and maids of high degree

Were dancing, holding one another's wrists ;

And the maidens wore fine raiment, and the youths

Tunics well-spun, glistering with olive-oil ;

The maidens all had chaplets, and the youths

Had dirks of gold, that hung by silver belts ;

And they at times ran round with nimble feet

Rapidly, like as when a potter sits

And tries with his hands a top, if it will spin ;

And then they ran in rows one after other.

And a great crowd stood round the pleasant band,

Delighted ; and among them there was singing

A bard divine to music of the lyre ;

And two men, very skilful in the dance,

Giving the time, were whirling in the midst.

    And last around the outer rim he placed

The great, broad river of Oceanus.

THE DEATH OF HECTOR.

So they the city through, as scared as hinds,

Wiped off the sweat, and drank and quench'd their thirst,

Leaning against the battlements, and the Greeks

Drew near, their shields across their shoulders slung.

But Fate bound Hector to remain outside,

In front of Ilium and the Scæan gates.

    Meanwhile Apollo to Achilles spake;

"Why with fleet feet, Achilles, dost pursue

Thou, mortal man, me, an immortal god?

Surely thou hast not yet perceived, that I

Am not of earth, so eager is thy haste.

Thou carest no more to slay the flying foe,

But, lo, they all are gather'd safe within

Their walls, while thou hast hither turn'd aside :
Me, who immortal am, thou canst not slay."

And, moved to wrath, Achilles, swift of foot,
Spake, " Archer-god, of gods most mischievous,
Thou didst me grievous wrong, to turn me now
Off from the wall; for many a man ere this
Had bitten the dust ere he reach'd Ilium.
Them hast thou saved, at cost of my renown ;
No wonder, seeing thou hadst nought to fear ;
Else, I would make thee pay me back in full. "

He spake ; and angry towards the city sped,
Rapidly, as in the chariot-race a steed
Runs swiftly at full stretch across the plain ;
So lightly wielded he his feet and limbs.

And him old Priam was the first to see,
Scouring the plain, and shining like the star,
That rises in the autumn, and whose rays
Are clearly seen among the stars at night ;
The star by men yclept Orion's hound ;
It is a bright star, but a sign of ill,

Portending fever to poor mortal men;

So, as he ran, the steel gleam'd on his breast.

    And the old man struck his forehead with his hands,

Raising his hands on high, and groan'd aloud,

Praying his son; but he before the gates

Stood, without flinching, resolute for the fight:

And thus with outstretch'd hands the old man pray'd:

    " Hector, my child, await not thou alone

This man, for fear thou quickly meet thine end,

Slain by him; for he is the mightier far.

Wretch! would he were no dearer to the gods

Than unto me; the vultures and the hounds

Would quickly have their prey, and from my heart

A load of sorrow were removed, for he

Hath me bereft of many goodly sons,

Slaying, or selling them in far off isles.

Yea now, when all are coop'd within the walls,

Two sons, born to me of Laothoe,

Lycaon and Polydorus, I nowhere see;

Now, if they still are living in the host,

With brass and gold we yet may ransom them;

For we have plenty, and Laothoe

Was by her royal father richly dower'd;

But, if they be already dead and gone,

'Twill be for grief to their mother and to me,

But greater far will be the grief of all,

If thou fall too beneath Pelides' hand:

So come, my son, within the walls, to save

Our men and matrons, and give not renown

To Achilles with the loss of thine own life.

Likewise on me, a most unhappy man,

Take pity, while I breathe the breath of life,

Whom ere long on the threshold of old age

The Father, son of Kronos, will destroy

Wretchedly, after seeing many woes,

My sons cut off, my daughters dragg'd away,

My home polluted, and my little ones

Dash'd cruelly to earth, and my sons' wives

Led away captive by the conquering Greeks:

And, last of all, when some one with a sword

Hath smitten me, or struck me with a spear,

And let my life out, then at mine own door

The greedy hounds will tear my corse, the hounds

I fed with mine own hands to keep my gates;

There they will lie, and eagerly lap my blood.

Now for a young man 'tis a seemly thing,

In battle slain and pierced by the sharp sword,

To lie exposed; for, now that he is dead,

All things are honourable, whate'er betide;

But, when the hair and beard is hoar with age,

To see the outraged corse of an old man,

This is the saddest sight beneath the sun."

The old man spake, and tore with both his hands

His hoary hair : but Hector was unmoved.

His mother also wept and made lament,

And pointing to her bosom with one hand

For Hector to regard, spake through her tears ;

"My son, respect this bosom, and if here

I nursed thee fondly in thy tender years,

Forget it not ; but keep this enemy off

Within our walls, nor meet him in the field.

Wretch! if he slay thee, mine own darling child,

I o'er thy bier shall never make lament,

I or thy dower'd wife; but far from us

The hounds shall tear thee by the Grecian ships."

So they twain weeping called unto their son,

Beseeching him; but Hector was unmoved;

And all the while the stately foe drew nigh.

And as a serpent, fed on venomous herbs,

Bides in its den the coming of a man;

And dreadful anger fills it, and it glares

Fearfully, as it rolls around its den;

So Hector, filled with might unquenchable,

Stood manfully his ground, and lean'd against

A jutting buttress his bright-shining shield;

And, deeply moved, spake thus to his own soul;

"Ah me! if I shall enter now the gates,

Polydamas will be the first to blame,

Who bade me lead the men within the walls

Last fatal night, when the great chief arose.

But I refused, though now it seems to me

It had been better to obey ; but now,

When through my folly many men have fallen,

I dread my townsmen and their long-robed dames,

For fear some one, a meaner man than I,

Should say, 'twas Hector's folly ruin'd all.

So will they speak, and then 'twere better far

Either victorious to return, or lie

Gloriously slain before my city's walls.

 " But were I now to lay upon the ground

My boss'd shield and my heavy helm, and go

Myself before the great Achilles' face ;

And promise to restore to the two sons

Of Atreus Helen and the precious things,

That Alexander in the hollow ships

Brought hitherward, the cause of all the strife ;

And to divide among the Grecian host

The substance of our city, and to bind

The people by a solemn oath to hide

Nought of their goods, but to divide them all ———

" But why thus idly commune with myself?

I fear me, should I go before him, he

Would shew me little pity or respect,

But slay me, as before him I should stand,

Just like a woman, helpless and unarm'd.

For he is, verily, not such an one,

As whom to speak withal in whispering tones

Under a tree or wall, as youth and maid,

As maid and youth speak whisperingly together.

" No : better to join battle ; and to see

Forthwith, to whether of the twain the sire

Olympian shall award the victory."

So stood he pondering ; and meanwhile drew near,

Like the great war-god, Enyalius,

Achilles ; o'er his shoulder, as he came,

Brandishing his great spear of Pelian ash,

Terrible ; and round about his armour gleamed,

Bright as a flame or as the rising sun.

A trembling came o'er Hector at the sight,

Nor had he courage longer to abide,

But left the gates behind, and fled away.

And Achilles after him rush'd furiously ;

Even as a hawk, the swiftest of all birds,

Upon the mountains lightly swoops adown

Upon a trembling dove, which underneath

Flies, and the hawk shrill shrieking close behind

Plunges into the brake to clutch the prey ;

So flew Achilles, and Hector fled in fear

Beneath the walls, and lightly moved his limbs.

So by the watch-tower and the windy tree,

The one wild fig-tree, ran they, evermore

By the beaten track close in beneath the walls.

And now they came unto the fountains fair,

Where rise the twin springs of the eddying stream,

Scamander : of the twain the one doth flow

With waters warm, and round about a smoke

Upriseth, like as from a burning fire ;

But the other floweth e'en in summer tide

With waters cold as hail, or snow, or ice ;

And close beside them were wide basins built,

Beautiful, of stone, where Trojan wives

And their fair daughters wash'd their raiment fine

Of old in peace-time, ere the Achæan came.

    Here ran they, one in front and one behind,

A brave man first, behind a braver far,

Rapidly ; nor strove they for an ox or skin,

Such as may win the runners in a race :

The prize they ran for was great Hector's life.

    And like as trampling horses in a race

Move swiftly round the goals, and the prize lies

For all to see, a tripod or a slave,

When men pay funeral honours to the dead ;

So thrice they twain around the walls of Troy

Ran swiftly ; and all the Gods were looking on ;

And among them spake the king of Gods and men ;

    " Ah me ! I see one chased around the walls,

One whom I love : my very heart is sore

For Hector, who so oft hath honour'd me

With sacrifice of oxen on the peaks

Of Ida many-valley'd, and in Troy

In the high places : now around the walls

Achilles, swift of foot, pursueth him.

Come therefore, Gods, bethink ye what to do,

Whether to rescue him, or let him fall

Beneath Achilles, brave man though he be."

    To him gray-eyed Athênê in reply :

" God of the thunder, dweller in the clouds,

Why, Father, what a word is this for thee !

A mortal man, by fate doom'd long ago,

Wouldst thou release from the stern bonds of death ?

So do ; but we are all of other mind."

    To her in answer cloud-compelling Zeus :

" Fear not, Tritogeneia, my own child ;

The words fell idly from me : I am will'd

To deal with thee in kindness ; so fulfil

What seemeth best to thee, sans let or fear."

    So spake he, and Athênê's eager heart

Was quicken'd to fresh eagerness, and away

From high Olympus she went swooping down.

    Meanwhile, unceasingly the chase went on ;

And as when on the mountains from its lair

A hound hath raised a fawn, and chaseth it

Through pass and glade, and if the flying fawn

For refuge cower into a brake, the hound

Runs on and on, until it track it out ;

So after Hector swift Achilles ran.

And evermore as Hector made to win

The gates right underneath the battlements,

So oft the other running in betimes

Turn'd him towards the plain ; for evermore

Fled Hector for the city ; and so it was,

As when one thinketh in a dream to run,

When whoso follows, never overtakes,

And whoso flees, seems never to escape ;

So 'twas with Hector and Æacides.

And maybe Hector had escaped his doom,

But that Apollo at the last drew nigh,

And made him stout of heart and lithe of limb.

    And now Achilles beckon'd with a nod

For all his people to hold back, nor hurl

A weapon, lest some other hand than his

Striking him won the glory of the deed.

But when the fourth time they had reach'd the springs,

Zeus took the golden balance in his hand,

And in the bowls thereof he placed two fates,

The fates of Hector and Æacides;

And poised the balance, and great Hector's fate

Outweigh'd the other, and sank down, down, down:

So Phœbus left him, and Athênê came

Beside Achilles, and spake winged words:

    "Now I do hope, Achilles, that we twain

Shall carry back great glory to the fleet,

When we have stripp'd the armour off the back

Of Hector, valiant soldier though he be.

For now, methinks, he hardly can escape

Our hands, for all the Archer-god may do,

Rolling himself before the feet of Zeus.

But rest thee for a while, and I will go

Yonder, and urge the man to stand and fight."

    She spake; and the hero glad at heart obey'd,

And leaning on his steel-tipt ashen spear
He stood; meanwhile the goddess went her way,
In voice and visage like Deiphobus,
And drawing close to Hector she thus spake:
" Good brother mine, Achilles swift of foot
Presseth thee sore indeed, around the walls
Chasing thee; but let us twain make a halt,
And break his onset, standing side by side."

    Him answer'd Hector of the glancing helm;
" Deiphobus, of all the children born
By Hecuba to Priam, heretofore
Thou hast been dearest unto me, but now
I needs must love thee with a tenfold love,
Because, though peril was before thine eyes,
For my sake thou hast ventured to the plain,
When all the rest are lingering within."

    To him gray-eyed Athênê in reply:
" Ah, brother, hadst thou seen how on their knees
Our father and good mother pray'd to me,
And how my comrades all join'd in the prayer,

To keep me in!—such terror held them all;

But on my breast there lay a load of shame.

So come, let us go forth, and let our spears

Find work to do, and let us know this day,

Whether yon prince shall bear our bloody spoils

To the ships, or fall himself beneath thy spear."

    So Pallas led him on with words of guile;

But when the heroes were now face to face,

Thus spake great Hector of the glancing helm;

"I will no longer flee before thy face,

Great son of Peleus; thrice around the walls,

Already have I run, nor dared to meet

Thine onset; now, my purpose is to stand,

And bide the issue, victory or death.

But come now, let us call the gods to be

Our witnesses, for they are best to guard

Such covenants as men make one with other.

I will not use thee ill, if Zeus to me

Shall give the victory, and I take thy life;

But, stripping off the armour, I will give

Thy body back; and deal thou so with me."

Achilles, scowling on him, made reply:
"Wretch, never speak of covenants with me;
Lions and men are never made sworn friends;
There is no peace betwixt the wolves and sheep,
But ill intent and enmity for ever:
So betwixt us no peace or love may be
Or covenant, till of the twain one fall
And with his life-blood sate the God of war.
So come, call all thy valour to thine aid;
Thou never had'st more need to prove thyself
A spearsman ready-handed, stout of heart;
Come, there is no escape; beneath my hand
Pallas Athênê soon shall lay thee low;
Then shalt thou pay in full for all the friends
In battle fall'n beneath thy ruthless spear."

He spake, and poising hurl'd the quivering shaft;
But Hector was in time to shun the blow,
For, seeing the spear a-coming, he crouch'd down,
And it flew over him, and the spear-head
Stuck in the ground: but Pallas caught it up,
And unobserved of Hector bare it back:

And thus spake Hector to Æacides:

" So, son of Peleus, thou hast miss'd thine aim;

It cannot be then, as thou saidst e'en now,

That Zeus hath given thee promise of my life;

Nay, but thy words were braggart lies, to make

Me frighten'd and forgetful of myself.

In me thou shalt not strike a coward's back,

But pierce me through the breast as I come on,

If the gods will it so: but now, beware

My spear—may the head be buried in thy heart,

For then the war were lighter to us all,

If thou wert fallen; thou, our deadliest bane."

He spake, and poising hurl'd the quivering spear.

That struck the middle of Pelides' shield,

And glanced off far away; and Hector stood

Angry, because the weapon from his hand

Had sped thus idly, and his visage fell;

For now he had no other spear to hurl;

So with a shout he call'd Deiphobus,

His brother of the white shield, to beg of him

His spear; but lo! Deiphobus was gone.

And Hector saw the end was come, and said;

" Now verily I see mine end is come:

I thought Deiphobus was at my side,

But he was safe behind the city's walls,

While Pallas in his shape beguilèd me.

So now the bitterness of death draws near,

And there is no escape; thus long ago

Methinks it hath seem'd good to Father Zeus,

And to the Archer-god, who heretofore

Have been my friends: but now my Fate is come:

But for all that I would not die without

Achievement of some glorious deed, to serve

For story to the men of after times."

He spake, and from the sheath the sharp sword drew,

That from his loins was swinging, great and strong;

And crouching down he made a swoop, as when

A soaring eagle through the murky clouds

Swoops down upon the plain to seize its prey,

A tender lamb or cow'ring leveret;

So Hector swoop'd, brandishing his sharp sword.

Achilles too rush'd on, his whole heart full

Of rage, and before his breast he held his shield

Of chased-work, beautiful; and over-head

His shining helm was nodding, and the plumes

Were streaming o'er his shoulders and around,

Plumes golden-yellow, which the Artist-god

Luxuriant had scatter'd on the helm.

And as among the stars at dead of night

Shines Hesperus, the fairest star in heaven,

So went a gleam from the sharp-pointed spear,

That great Achilles wielded, vowing death

To Hector, and scanning all his form to find

Where best his armour would let in a wound.

But Hector's body was all cased in mail,

The shining mail from off Patroclus torn;

Only between the shoulders and the neck,

There where a wound is mortal, might be seen

An opening, and thereat Achilles aim'd,

And through the soft flesh the sharp spear-point drave;

The wind-pipe was untouch'd, so for a while

The power of speech was left the wounded man:

Down in the dust he fell, and over him
In triumph the great son of Peleus spake :

    " Hector, when thou wert stripping of his arms
The dead Patroclus, thou did'st think to pass
Unpunish'd, nor hadst thou a thought of me.
Fool ! by the hollow ships was left behind
A swordsman far more terrible than he,
Myself, thy victor: so this body of thine
To dogs and birds shall be a prey, but him
The Greeks shall bear with honour to his grave."

    And faintly breathing, Hector made reply:
" Achilles, I entreat thee by thy life
And parents dear, let not my body lie
A prey to the dogs beside the Grecian ships ;
But take for ransom what of brass and gold
My father and good mother will freely give ;
And send my body home, that it may be
By men of mine own city and their wives
Laid with due honour on the funeral pyre."

    And scowling on him, spake Æacides :
" Dog, never pray to me; for would to heaven

The fury in my heart would let me tear
Thy body piecemeal and devour it raw;
Such little chance hath any to release
Thy body, though before me they should bring
A tenfold ransom or a twentyfold;
Should Priam offer to redeem thy corse
With its own weight in gold, not for it all
Should thine own mother lay thee on the bier,
And weep above thee; no, the dogs and birds
Shall tear thy body piecemeal, limb by limb."

And dying, Hector slowly made reply:
" I knew it would be so; my chance was poor
To move thee, for thy heart is hard as stone.
Beware, lest unto thee I prove a curse,
That day when Paris and the Archer-god
With arrow from the string shall lay thee low,
For all thy valour, by the Scæan gates."

He spake: the death-film gather'd o'er his eyes,
And the soul to Hades from the body fled,
Mourning its fate, and loth to leave behind
Beauty and vigour and manhood in its prime.

And prince Achilles thus address'd the dead :
" Die thou, and I will welcome mine own fate
When Zeus so wills it, and the Gods above."

He spake, and from the body wrench'd the spear,
And cast it by, and stripp'd the bloody arms
From off the shoulders of the dead : meanwhile
The Grecian soldiers all came flocking round,
To catch a glimpse of the grand, stately form
Of Hector ; nor came one but gave a wound ;
And thus they spake, the one unto the other :

" Hector is safer now to deal withal,
By heavens, than when he set the ships a-blaze."

So spake they, and struck the body as it lay ;
But when the armour was stripp'd off the corse,
Up stood Achilles, and spake wingèd words :

" Leaders and councillors of the host, give ear ;
The Gods have given into our hands this man,
Who did us more of mischief than they all,
Wherefore let us in harness make essay
What may the will be of his countrymen ;
Whether, now he is fallen, they choose to leave

Their battlements, or whether they are bent

To hold their ground, though Hector is no more.

But why hold converse thus with mine own soul ?

By the ships there lies unwept, unsepultur'd,

The dead Patroclus ; him will I not forget,

The while I live, and while my limbs can move.

For though in Hades they forget the dead,

I even there will yet remember him.

So raise the song of triumph, and return

Bearing the body to the hollow ships :

We have won glory ; we have slain the prince,

To whom they pray'd as to a God in Troy."

　　　He spake ; and meditated usage foul

To Hector ; for the tendons of both feet

Between the ankle and the heel he pierc'd,

And fasten'd thongs of leather thereunto,

And bound him to the car, and let the head

Trail on the ground, and stepp'd upon the car,

And lifted up the splendid spoils, and smote

The steeds to gallop, and away they flew :

And as the corse was trail'd along, the dust

Rose underneath, and the dark, glossy hair

Was scatter'd in the dust, and in the dust

Was dragg'd the face, afore so beautiful—

For Zeus had granted to his mortal foes

Thus to dishonour him in his own dear land.

And while the face was trailing in the dust,

His mother saw her child, and tore her hair,

And far away from her with both hands flung

Her shining head-dress, and shriek'd out aloud ;

And piteously his father groan'd, and all

The town was fill'd with wailing and shrill cries ;

And it was even as though Ilium

From crown to base were smouldering in fire.

And the old man, utterly distraught with woe,

Scarcely by force was held within the gates ;

Down in the mire he roll'd, and pray'd to all,

Each one by name, to let him issue forth :

" Hold, friends ; for all you love me, let me go

Out of the city to the Grecian ships ;

Let me entreat this cruel man of blood ;

It may be he will reverence mine age,

And pity my grey hairs ; for surely he

Hath even such a father as myself,

Old Peleus, who begat and rear'd him up,

A curse to Troy—a very curse to me,

For all my stout sons fall'n beneath his hand :

But for them all I do not grieve so much,

With all my sorrow, as for one, whose loss

Will bring my grey hairs swiftly to the grave,

For Hector—would he had died within mine arms ;

Then had we wept the fulness off our hearts,

His mother and I, a most unhappy twain."

So spake he, weeping ; and his countrymen

Gave groan for groan ; meanwhile, among her maids

Queen Hecuba led on the long lament :

" Me miserable, what shall I do, my child,

Now thou art gone ! for thou wast night and day

My glory, and a blessing unto all

The men and women-folk that lived in Troy ;

And when thou camest from the war, they gave

Thee welcome such as men give to a god ;

And thou wast unto them a crown of joy,

In life ; but now the fated end is come."

    Weeping she spake ; but Hector's wife as yet

Knew nought of all, for none had made her ware

How Hector tarried yet without the walls ;

But she was weaving in an inner room

An ample cloth of purple, and tracing it

With flowers and many-hued embroideries ;

And she had bidden her long-hair'd maids to place

Upon the fire a tripod, and prepare

A bath for Hector when he left the field :

Poor simple one ; she little thought, alas !

How Pallas by the great Achilles' hand

Had sent her Hector far away, where baths

Would needless be henceforth for evermore.

And meanwhile from the battlements there came

The sound of lamentation and shrill cries ;

The shuttle fell from her hands, and her knees shook,

And mid her long-hair'd maidens she thus spake :

    " Hither come two of you, and let me see

What thing hath happen'd ; for methought I heard

The voice of our good mother, and my limbs

Are frozen, and I have a boding fear,

Some mischief hath befallen a prince of Troy.

Heaven grant it be not so ; but still I fear

Lest Hector, sever'd from the walls, is driven

Before the great Achilles towards the plain ;

And lest that gallant spirit, over bold,

Be quench'd this day ; for he was ne'er content

To bide his turn, but yielding place to none

Ever kept first and foremost in the van."

    She spake, and follow'd by her maids rush'd out,

Wild as a Mænad, her heart beating fast ;

But when they reach'd the ramparts and the crowd,

She stood and eagerly gaz'd towards the plain,

And there she saw the body of her lord

Dragg'd onwards, and the swift steeds dragging it

Recklessly at full gallop to the sea.

And down upon her eyes the black night came,

And falling backwards she swoon'd out her life,

And from her head the shining head-gear fell,

The band and coif and woven anadem,

And the veil, that golden Aphrodite gave,

That day when Hector of the glancing helm

Led her away from her old father's home,

A queenly wife and with a queenly dower.

And all her royal sisterhood flock'd round,

Comforting her, and kept the life within;

But when her spirit was reviv'd, and back

Her senses came, she heav'd a long-drawn sigh,

And thus among the women-folk she spake:

"O Hector, woe is me! so with one fate

We twain were born; thou in the Trojan home

Of Priam; I in Thebes beneath the woods

Of Placus, in the home of my old sire,

Eëtion, who from childhood rear'd me up

Unto a fate unhappy as his own!

O would to God I never had been born!

Now in the darkness of the under-world

Methinks thou wilt be journeying to the home

Of Hades, but thou leavest me to mourn,

A widow-woman; and the boy, we twain

Had born to us, is but a little child;

And thou in death, dear Hector, wilt not prove

A blessing unto him, nor he to thee ;

For e'en if he escape the chance of war,

Trouble awaits him in the coming years ;

His heritage will pass to other hands ;

For the orphan child stands utterly desolate

Among his fellows ; and he will go betimes

In need of somewhat to his father's friends,

And catch one by the tunic or the cloak ;

And maybe one in pity will just deign

To hold a goblet out to wet his lips,

And nothing more ; and maybe at a feast

Some fellow, that hath living parents twain,

Will jostle him, or smite him on the cheek,

Or speak these words of bitterest reproach—

'Brat, get thee gone ; thy father sups not here.'

And weeping to his widow'd mother's lap

He will return—my boy, Astyanax,

Who sat upon his father's knee, and fared

On marrow only and fatlings of the lea ;

My boy, who, when his fun had tired him out,

Slept in a soft bed, in his nurse's arms,

His heart filled to the brim with happiness ;

And many a time will he be made to feel

His loss—Astyanax, the hope of Troy,

For so men call'd him—rightly called, for thou

Wert aye the safeguard of their gates and walls.

But far away from home, by the beak'd ships

Upon thy body, when the dogs have had

Their meal, the crawling worms will feed ; on thee

Naked, for all thy raiment lieth here,

Fine, beautiful, the work of ladies' hands ;

But wherein shall it profit thee ? thy limbs

Will ne'er be wrapp'd therein : nay, I will burn

It all, and the burning of it shall be held

For honour to thee in the sight of all

The men and women of thine own dear Troy."

 So spake she, weeping ; and the women all

Took up the lamentation, groan for groan.

THE FLIGHT OF PERSEUS WITH THE GORGON'S HEAD,

AND

THE TRANSFORMATION OF ATLAS.

———◆———

Hence through the empty air by warring winds
Tost hither and thither, like a rainy cloud,
He speeds along, and from his dizzy height
Looks down, as he flies over the wide world.
Three times he visited the frozen North ;
Three times the stars that shine on Southern seas ;
Again from West to East, from East to West
The windy currents waft him, till at length,
As day was setting, fearful of the dark
He lighted down upon Hesperian land,
The realm of ancient Atlas : here he sought

A shelter for the coming night, until
The Morning-Star should wake the slumbering fires,
And bring again the chariot of the Dawn.

  Here Atlas dwelt, son of Iapetus,
In stature tallest of all mortal men,
King of the western world's remotest rim,
And of the sea, into whose cooling waves,
Tired with their long day's journey through the sky,
The panting horses of the Sun-god plunge.
For him a thousand flocks, a thousand herds
Roam'd in the pastures ; and no neighbour mark'd
With boundary line his solitary realm.
His were the orchards of the wondrous trees,
With fruit and leaves and branches all of gold.

  " Stranger," thus Perseus to the monarch spake,
" If noble birth have any claim on thee,
My father is the king of Gods and men ;
If thou art touch'd with deeds of high emprise,
Thy heart may well be touch'd by deeds of mine :
I beg a night's rest only."   Hereupon

The king remember'd the old prophecy,

By Themis on Parnassus given of yore :

" Atlas" so Themis spake, "the day will come

To see the gold stript off thy trees ; a son

Of Jove shall have the honour of the spoil."

Wherefore the king had girt his garden round

With solid walls, and set a dragon-guard,

And banish'd every stranger from his realms.

So then to Perseus he replied : " Begone,

Or else thou'lt find thy lies avail not here

Of lofty deeds and heavenly father-hood."

And not content with menace, he essay'd

Rude violence ; the while the other made

Resistance, firm but temperate withal :

His strength at last gave way ; for who in strength

Could vie with Atlas ? and so Perseus spake ;

" Seeing thou reck'st so little of my love,

Take thy reward ;" and shading his own eyes,

Stretched forth his left arm, and exposed to view

The snaky tresses of the Gorgon's head.

Big as he was, Atlas to mountain turn'd :

His hair and beard pass into shaggy woods ;

His shoulders into ridges stretch away ;

Where was his head, is now a mountain-peak ;

His bones to granite change.   On every side

He grows and grows past measure, till the heaven

Reposes on him with its weight of stars.

CERES AND PROSERPINE.

———◆———

CYANE, THE WATER-NYMPH.

There is not far from Henna's walls a pool,

Pergus by name, of waters deep and cool ;

Cayster, its melodious banks along,

With all its swans, is not more rife with song ;

Woods, to the water's edge stretch'd round about,

With leafy curtain shut the noon-day out ;

Flowers of all hues abound, and branches fling

A coolness out, that makes perpetual spring.

'Twas in this valley Proserpine was straying,

With a sweet band of little maids a-maying,

In baskets or their laps a-gathering posies

Of lilies white, dark violets and roses ;

Proserpine's only thought and only care

Was that her lap should be the fullest there :

Pluto beheld, loved, seized the maid away

At once—so little brook'd his love delay.

Upon her mother and her friends for aid,

Her mother loudest, shriek'd the frightened maid ;

Her robe was rent, and fluttering in the wind,

As flew the chariot, fell the flowers behind ;

But e'en amid her wonderment and fears

This simple loss called forth her childish tears.

Away, away the flying chariot speeds ;

The royal lover cheers the panting steeds ;

Over their necks, over their streaming manes

He bends and loosely hangs the violet reins ;

By the deep lakes and standing pools he flies,

Where sulphurous vapours through the rifts uprise ;

Until they reach the city by the sea,

By princes built of ancient Ephyre.

　　There is 'twixt Cyane and the Pisan rill

A narrow strip of water deep and still ;

There dwelt beneath this pool, that bore her name,

Cyane, a Naiad of Sicilian fame.

It so befell that, as the car drew near,

The Nymph was rising from her waters clear;

She saw, and recognised the God, and cried:

" Hold in thy steeds; if thou would'st win the
      bride,

Her mother Ceres will with right demand

Courteous entreaty and not force of hand.

If little things with great ones may compare,

I in love matters too have had my share;

But not with violence Anapis strove,

He, like a lover, woo'd and won my love."

    She spake, and stretch'd her arms to bar his path;

No longer could the God restrain his wrath;

He lash'd his terrible steeds, and with a swing

Hurled his huge sceptre to the lowermost spring;

A cavern yawned, and into realms of night

Chariot and charioteer plunged out of sight.

    Her fount despised, her mistress stolen away

To brooding sorrow leave the nymph a prey;

She pines and pines, and where she late bare rule,

Melting in tears, is lost in her own pool ;

Her limbs grow soft and softer every one,

Supple and suppler each resisting bone ;

Her hands and feet and every part extreme

First disappear to mingle with the stream ;

Her face, her neck, her shoulders, and her breast

Little by little melt into the rest ;

The liquid gradual spreads through pores and veins,

And nothing you could touch or grasp remains.

CERES AND PROSERPINE.

CERES AND THE RUDE BOY.

Over the wide earth and the wider main
The trembling mother sought her child in vain ;
Aurora, as with dripping locks she came,
Found her at work, and Hesperus the same ;
A pine-torch on Mount Ætna from a spark
She lit, and bore it restless through the dark :
Again, when daylight drove the stars away,
She search'd from sun-rise to the close of day ;
Wearied with toil, with lips athirst and dry,
She look'd in vain some cheering spring to spy ;
At length she sees a lonely straw-thatched shed ;
She knocks, and out an old crone pokes her head,
Who gives of porridge from her scanty store ;
Poor stuff, perhaps, but she had nothing more.

The Goddess sups it eagerly, the while

A lad looks on with a provoking smile :

" Why, from the way she eats her dinner, Mother,

You'd think she never hoped to have another."

The Goddess took offence, as who would not ?

And punish'd the offender on the spot :

To take an aim she just drew back a pace,

Then flung the porridge in the urchin's face ;

With pimples straight the face was mottled o'er,

And wee legs grew, where arms had grown before ;

Down on all fours he grovelled, and a tail

Behind him on the ground was seen to trail ;

For fear the imp should mischief find to do,

His shape was shrivelled to an inch or two ;

His mother shriek'd, and tried in vain, poor soul,

To clutch him, but he slipped into a hole ;

In lizard-shape his after life he spent,

A warning to all boys on mischief bent,

Whene'er they meet respectable old dames,

Not to make faces or give vulgar names.

CERES AND PROSERPINE.

———◆———

PROSERPINE AND THE STORY-TELLER.

There is, so stories tell, in Elis found
A little stream, that sinks into the ground,
And with fresh waters runs beneath the sea,
Until it reaches far-off Sicily.
This under-ground and under-water way
Swam Arethuse, a water-nymph, one day,
And down below in Pluto's realm she spied
The lost one, Proserpine, a queen and bride.
The happy tidings she to Ceres brings,
Who straight her flight up to Olympus wings,
And eloquent with all a mother's love,
Pleads her hard case before the throne of Jove ;
The father answered—but the words he said
Gave little hope, and not a little dread—

" Pluto and Neptune, my two brothers, and I

Are Lords of Hades and the Sea and Sky :

Thy Proserpine is queen of one of these ;

If this content thee not, thou'rt hard to please :

Still, if this honour seems mere banishment,

And thou on her return art fully bent,

On this condition I will grant thy prayer,

If she have never broken fast down there."

Now Proserpine, it chanced, that very day,

Through Pluto's garden went her lonely way,

And, tired and hardly knowing what to do,

Pluck'd a pomegranate, and ate a grain or two :

The only witness unto what was done

Was child of Orphnê and of Acheron,

The lad Ascalaphus ; provoking elf,

He might have kept the secret to himself ;

The little story-teller told it all,

And Proserpine was fixed beyond recall :

The harm was done, and nothing could undo it,

But the offender had good cause to rue it.

Weeping and praying and wringing both his
    hands,
Before the angry queen the culprit stands ;
She lifts a handful from the Stygian flood
Of muddy water or of watery mud,
And after a few words of magic said,
Scatters the liquid on the wretch's head.

    His little snub-nose sharpens to a beak ;
A fluffy down spreads gradual o'er his cheek ;
Into his head one half his body flies,
And from his head stare out two big round eyes ;
With painful effort lazily he swings
His arms beneath the novel weight of wings ;
His little toes to crooked talons bend,
And feathers cover him from end to end ;
In fact he stands an Owl ; in other words,
The ugliest, unluckiest of birds.

LATONA AND THE RUSTICS.

Latona, from her isle of Delos driven,

Was flying from the jealous Queen of heaven :

Close to her breast, wrapt in her mantle's fold,

She clasped her twins, a very few days old :

At length with toil and heat she thirsty grew ;

Her little ones were very thirsty too ;

But still, with parchèd lips and aching feet.

She push'd on bravely through the noon-day heat ;

Until she spies beneath a neighbouring hill

A pool of water, fresh, and green, and still :

Now I suppose the dwellers in this vale

Made baskets, chairs, and wicker-work for sale,

For crowds of men and women o'er the meads

Were gathering rushes, willow-slips, and reeds ;

Onwards the Goddess came, and by the brink

Kneeled down upon the grass, and stooped to drink ;

The rustics pulled her with rude hands away,

While she in her sore need deigned thus to pray :

" Wherefore, good friends, so churlish as decline

A share of what is no more yours than mine ?

Why, surely, rich and poor alike may share

These common blessings, water, light, and air :

Give me, I beg and pray for pity's sake,

What without begging I have right to take :

Why, for your pool, I have no wish, heaven knows,

To wash therein my hands, or face, or clothes ;

I only ask to drink ; why should you fear

'Twould make the water shallower or less clear ?

Have pity ; see, how tired I am and weak ;

My lips and tongue are dry ; I scarce can speak :

Water, or I shall faint : one quaff divine

To me were fresher, sweeter than all wine :

Give me one draught, then, and I'll own, to you,

Next after Father Jove, my life is due :

If me you pity not, I pray you spare

These pets, who, look you, stretch their hands in

  prayer."

  Strange ; at the word, as though it understands,

Each child holds out its silly little hands ;

A prayer so eloquent, a sight so pretty

Might well have moved a heart of stone to pity :

These clowns had hearts, then, harder than a stone ;

Their gentle suppliant they bid begone ;

Some call her names ; some push her from the place

Some shake their dirty fists in her poor face ;

Some spiteful wretches in the water wallow,

Till 'tis unfit for any pig to swallow.

  Latona's patience fairly went at last ;

Fatigue and thirst both into anger past :

Disdaining further words of supplication,

She burst into this sudden execration :

" Be it your lot, abominable rabble,

For ever in the mud to splash and dabble."

She spake ; and in a twinkling on the green

A swarm of speckled frogs were hopping seen ;

Doomed by the Fates to lead a life for ever

Amphibious in marsh, or pond, or river ;

Their voices roughen'd, and, whene'er they spoke,

The only sound they made was "croak! croak!
    croak !"

Their heads and bodies touch'd ; no neck was seen ;

Their stomachs were all white ; their back was
    green ;

A hump was there, where necks had been before ;

Their mouths stretch'd out, till they would stretch
    no more.

And, had you seen, you would have thought it
    strange,

That habits could with form so quickly change :

Some in the pool kept swimming at the top,

Some from the bank dived right in with a plop ;

Some sat, as if on serious thought intent,

Some in and out frisk'd to their heart's content ;

But, though their lives were now in water past,

L

Their old bad ways clung by them to the last ;

The water never drown'd that quarrelling spirit,

Which all their children to this day inherit,

Who still are thought, e'en in this generation,

The crossest, croakingest creatures in creation.

DANAE AND CHILD IN THE ARK.

When in the ark of curious workmanship
The winds and swaying waters fearfully
Were rocking her, with streaming eyes around
Her boy the mother threw her arms, and said,

   "O darling, I am very miserable ;
But thou art cosy-warm and sound asleep
In this thy dull, close-cabin'd prison-house,
Stretched at full ease in the dark, ebon gloom.
Over thine head of long and tangled hair
The wave is rolling ; but thou heedest not,
Nor heedest thou the noises of the winds,
Wrapt in thy purple cloak, sweet pretty one.

   "But if this fearful place had fears for thee,
Those little ears would listen to my words ;
But sleep on, baby, and let the sea-waves sleep,
And sleep our own immeasurable woes.
O Father Zeus, I pray some change may come ;
But, Father, if my words are over-bold,
Have pity, and for the child's sake pardon me."

STATIUS; THEBAIS. II. 32-42.

Est locus (Inachiæ dixerunt Tænara gentes),

Quâ formidatum Maleæ spumantis in auras

It caput, et nullos admittit culmine visus.

Stat sublimis apex, ventosque imbresque serenus

Despicit, et tantum fessis insiditur astris.

Illic exhausti posuêre cubilia venti;

Fulminibusque iter est: medium cava nubila montis

Insumsêre latus: summos nec præpetis alæ

Plausus adit colles, nec rauca tonitrua pulsant;

Ast, ubi prona dies, longos super æquora fines

Exigit, atque ingens medio natat umbra profundo.

CAPE MATAPAN.

There is a spot, named in Inachian lands
Tænarus, where foaming Malea's dreaded cape
Rises in air beyond the ken of man.
Sublime the peak on winds and rains serene
Looks down ; above, the weary stars alone.
There the tired winds have made their resting-place,
And lightnings fly ; upon the mountain's waist
Hollow clouds hover ; on the topmost heights
Nor swift wing flaps, nor rumbling thunders beat ;
But, when day falls, he stretches far away.
And his huge shadow swims i' the central deep.

STATIUS; THEBAIS. I. 303-311.

Paret Atlantiades dictis genitoris; et inde
Summa pedum properè plantaribus illigat alis,
Obnubitque comas, et temperat astra galero.
Tum dextræ virgam inseruit, quâ pellere dulces
Aut suadere iterum somnos, quâ nigra subire
Tartara, et exsangues animare assueverat umbras.
Desiluit; tenuique exceptus inhorruit aurâ.
Nec mora, sublimes raptim per inane volatus
Carpit, et ingenti designat nubila gyro.

THE DESCENT OF MERCURY.

Hermes obeys his sire's commands, and straight

In haste with wingèd sandals binds his feet,

And veils his locks and caps his starry head.

Then takes in hand the wand, wherewith he wont

To banish or to bring again sweet sleep,

To enter Hell and charm the bloodless shades : ʒ

Down he leaps, rustling, caught i' the thin air,

And rapidly through the void his flight sublime

He wings, and with a halo marks the clouds.

STATIUS; SILVÆ. V. 5. 79-87.

Nonne gemam te, care puer? quo sospite, natos
Non cupii: primo gremium cui protinus ortu
Applicui fixique meum: cui verba sonosque
Monstravi, questusque et murmura cæca resolvens;
Reptantemque solo, demissus ad oscula, dextrâ
Erexi; blandique sinus jam jamque natantes
Excepisse genas, dulcesque arcessere somnos;
Cui nomen vox prima meum, ludusque tenello
Risus, et e nostro veniebant gaudia vultu.

ON THE DEATH OF A CHILD.

Shall I not mourn thee, darling boy? with whom

Childless I miss'd not children of my own;

I, who first caught and pressed thee to my breast,

And call'd thee mine, and taught thee sounds and

    words,

And solved the riddle of thy murmurings,

And stoop'd to catch thee creeping on the ground,

And propp'd thy steps, and ever had my lap

Ready, if drowsy were those little eyes,

To rock them with a lullaby to sleep:

Thy first word was my name, thy fun my smile,

And not a joy of thine but came from me.

STATIUS ; SILVÆ. II. (4).

Huc doctæ stipentur aves, queis nobile fandi

Jus Natura dedit: plangat Phœbeïus ales,

Auditasque memor penitus demittere voces

Sturnus, et Aonio versæ certamine picæ,

Quique refert jungens iterata vocabula perdix,

Et quæ Bistonio queritur soror orba cubili.

Ferte simul gemitus, cognataque ducite flammis

Funera; et hoc cunctæ miserandum addiscite carmen:

  Occidit, aëriæ celeberrima gloria gentis,

Psittacus, ille plagæ viridis regnator Eoæ;

Quem non gemmatâ volucris Junonia caudâ

Vinceret adspectu, gelidi non Phasidis ales,

Nec quas humenti Numidæ rapuêre sub Austro.

Ille salutator regum, nomenque locutus

POOR POLL.

Hither come all ye learned birds, to whom
Nature hath given the noble right of speech :
Come, raven, bird by Phœbus changed of old,
Come, mimic starlings and transformèd pies,
Come, chirping partridge and sad nightingale :
Weep all, and lay your brother in his grave,
And sing with me this melancholy dirge—
    Dead is the glory of the aërial race,
Poll, the green monarch of an Eastern clime ;
Whom neither Juno's bird of starry tail
Rivall'd, nor he from Phasis, chilly stream ;
Nor birds of Afric, caught where Auster rains :
The pet of kings, who knew great Cæsar's name,
Who had his words of fun or mimic plaint,

Cæsareum, et queruli quondam vice functus amici ;

Nunc conviva levis, monstrataque reddere verba

Tam facilis ; quo tu, Melior dilecte, recluso,

Nunquam solus eras.   At non inglorius umbris

Mittitur: Assyrio cineres adolentur amomo ;

Et tenues Arabum respirant gramina plumæ,

Sicaniosque crocos: senio nec fessus inerti

Scandit odoratos Phœnix felicior ignes.

The rogue, to cheer his master's lonely hours.

Ah ! not inglorious to the shades he goes ;

With Syrian spice his ashes are embalm'd,

His plumage fine breathes gums of Araby

And saffron of Sicilia ; not more blest

The bird, who, tired with immortality,

Climbs ever and anon his odorous pyre.

STATIUS; THEBAIS. I. 364.

Ille tamen (modo saxa jugis fugientia ruptis

Miratus, modo nubigenas e montibus amnes

Aure pavens, passimque insano turbine raptas

Pastorum pecorumque domos) non segnius, amens,

Incertusque viæ per nigra silentia vastum

Haurit iter: pulsat metus undique, et undique frater.

Ac velut hiberno deprensus navita ponto,

Cui neque temo piger, neque amico sidere monstrat

Luna vias, medio cœli pelagique tumultu

Stat rationis inops: jam jamque aut saxa malignis

Exspectat submersa vadis, aut vertice acuto

Spumantes scopulos erectæ incurrere proræ:

Talis, opaca legens nemorum, Cadmeïus heros

Accelerat, vasto metuenda umbone ferarum

Excutiens stabula, et prono virgulta refringit

Pectore (dat stimulos animo vis mœsta timoris),

Donec ab Inachiis victâ caligine tectis

Emicuit, lucem devexa in mœnia fundens,

Larissæus apex.

POLYNICES IN THE STORM.

Onwards he goes, listening in wonderment
As stones come tumbling down the mountain-sides,
And rain-swoln torrents sweep away the homes
Of sheep and shepherd ; onward still he goes
Through gloom and silence on his lonely way,
Not knowing where he goes ; his heart beats fast ;
His brother's image dogs him at each step.
And as a sailor tempest-caught at sea,
Without or polar star or friendly moon
To guide, in warring of the sea and sky
Is utterly perplex'd, and evermore
Thinketh to founder on a perilous reef,
Or run his prow against sharp-pointed rocks ;
So Polynices threading the dark wood
Hurries, and with the great boss of his shield
Disturbs the lair of beasts, and presses on
Snapping the brushwood—such his haste and fear—
Till from afar through waning darkness shone,
With light upon its sloping battlements,
The castle of Larissa.

CLAUDIAN ; RAPT. PROS., I. 253.

Nec color unus inest: stellas accendit in auro;

Ostro fundit aquas; attollit litora gemmis,

Filaque mentitos jamjam cælantia fluctus

Arte tument: credas illidi cautibus algam,

Et raucum bibulis inserpere murmur arenis.

Addit quinque plagas: mediam subtemine rubro

Obsessam fervore notat: squalebat adustus

Limes, et assiduo sitiebant stamina sole:

Vitales utrimque duas; quas mitis oberrat

Temperies, habitanda viris: tum fine supremo

Torpentes traxit geminas, brumâque perenni

Fœdat, et æterno contristat frigore telas.

CERES' EMBROIDERY.

A work it was of rare device ; the stars
In gold she lit ; dark-blue the waters roll'd ;
With pearl the shore is raised, and evermore
The embroider'd threads swell into mimic waves ;
You see the sea-weed tumbling on the rocks,
You hear the hoarse sea roar along the sand.
Five zones she adds ; whereof with scarlet thread
The central zone she weaves ; the track adust
Bakes on the web beneath continual suns ;
On either side with temperate air serene
Two, fit for life and the abode of man ;
Then on the outer edge the torpid belts
She draws, and dims the beauty of her work
With ice eternal and eternal cold.

CLAUDIAN ; RAPT. PROS., I. 274.

Merserat unda diem: sparso nox humida somno

Languida cœruleis invexerat otia bigis.

Jamque viam Pluton superas molitur ad auras,

Germani monitu: torvos invisa jugales

Alecto temone ligat, qui pascua mandunt

Cocyti, spatiisque Erebi nigrantibus errant ;

Stagnaque tranquillæ potantes marcida Lethes,

Ægra soporatis spumant oblivia linguis:

Orphnæus crudele micans, Æthonque sagittâ

Ocyor, et Stygii sublimis gloria Nycteus

Armenti, Ditisque notâ signatus Alastor,

Stabant ante fores juncti, sævumque fremebant,

Crastina venturæ spectantes gaudia prædæ

THE CHARIOT OF PLUTO.

The Sun had sunk i' the waves, and dewy Night

On car of ebony had brought repose.

Now sets out Pluto on his upward way,

At Jove's behest : his chariot-steeds are yoked

By fell Alecto ; dreadful steeds, that feed

On plains of Erebus by Cocytus' banks,

Whose lips are froth'd with Lethe's stagnant tide,

Lethe, the river of Oblivion.

Orphnœus wildly glaring, Æthon swift

As arrow, Alastor mark'd with Pluto's brand,

And Nycteus, glory of the Stygian herd,

Were standing at the gate, and neighing fierce,

With eager longing for the morrow's prey.

CLAUDIAN; PHŒNIX.

Oceani summo circumfluus æquore lucus
Trans Indos Eurumque viret, qui primus anhelis
Sollicitatur equis; vicinaque verbera sentit,
Humida roranti resonant cum limina curru,
Unde rubet ventura dies, longeque coruscis
Nox afflata rotis refugo pallescit amictu.
Hæc fortunatus nimium Titanius ales
Regna colit; Solisque plagâ defensus iniquâ,
Possidet intactas ægris animantibus oras;
Sæva nec humani patitur contagia mundi;
Par volucer Superis; stellas qui vividus æquat
Durando, membrisque terit redeuntibus ævum;
Non epulis saturare famem, non fontibus ullis
Assuetus prohibere sitim: sed purior illum
Solis fervor alit; ventosaque pabula libat
Tethyos, innocui carpens alimenta vaporis.

THE PHŒNIX.

Rimm'd by the waters of Oceanus
There blooms a grove beyond far Eastern Ind,
Trod by the panting steeds of morn, and feels
The neighbouring rays, when 'neath the dewy car
The gates of morning echo, and the day
Blushes, and far before the shining wheels
Night's gradual robe of darkness pales away.
Here dwells Apollo's bird supremely blest,
Far from extremes of heat or cold, in realms
To miserable mortals all unknown.
He knows no contact with the world of man,
The bird divine ; but like the eternal stars
Lives on with limbs unconscious of decay.
No banquets feed him, and no watery springs
Assuage his thirst ; his food aerial
Is sunlight pure and vapour of the sea.

CLAUDIAN; RAPE OF PROSERPINE, I. 76-88.

Tum Maiâ genitum, qui fervida dicta reportet,

Imperat acciri.   Cyllenius adstitit ales

Somniferam quatiens virgam, tectusque galero.

Ipse rudi fultus solio, nigrâque verendus

Majestate sedet: squalent immania fœdo

Sceptra situ; sublime caput mœstissima nubes

Asperat; et diræ riget inclementia formæ.

Terrorem dolor augebat.   Tum talia celso

Ore tonat: (tremefacta silent, dicente tyranno,

Atria; latratum triplicem compescuit ingens

Janitor; et presso lacrymarum fonte resedit

Cocytos, tacitisque Acheron obmutuit undis,

Et Phlegethonteæ requiêrunt murmura ripæ.)

PLUTO.

He bids them summon Maia's son to bear

His angry message.   Hermes at the word

Came, wing'd and capp'd, with drowsy wand in hand.

On his rude throne in grim and awful state

The monarch sits ; upon his front sublime

A cloud of sorrow gathers, and his form

Dreadful is yet more dreadful in his woe.

Then, as in thundering tones he speaks, the hall

Trembling is silent, and huge Cerberus

Holds in his triple bark ; Cocytus stays

His fount of tears, and Acheron is still,

And still the murmuring banks of Phlegethon.

CATULLUS; FUNUS PASSERIS.

Passer mortuus est meæ puellæ,

Passer deliciæ meæ puellæ,

Nam mellitus erat, suamque nôrat

Ipsam tam bene quam puella matrem ;

Nec sese a gremio illius movebat,

Sed solam ad dominam usque pipilabat :

Qui nunc it per iter tenebricosum

Illuc unde negant redire quenquam.

O factum male ! O miselle passer !

Tuâ nunc operâ meæ puellæ

Flendo turgiduli rubent ocelli.

THE DEAD CANARY.

Wee bit birdie's dead and gane,
    The pet o' my ain dearie O,
And now is journeyin' all alane
    The road so dark and dreary O,
The road that maun be trod by all
    O' mortal men and birdies O.

Sweet birdie kenn'd his mistress weel,
    Her face fra ilka ither O,
As weel as e'er my lassie kenn'd
    The face o' her ain mither O,
And nestled in her breast, he'd pipe
    And cheep the hour thegither O.

Ah birdie, what for was thy life,
    Thy puir bit life sae fleetin' O,
'Tis a' for thee my dearie's een
    Are red and sair wi' greetin' O,
'Tis a' for thee thae bonny een
    Are red and sair wi' greetin' O.

x

STATIUS; SILVÆ. V. 14.

Crimine quo merui juvenis, placidissime Divûm,

Quove errore miser, donis ut solus egerem,

Somne, tuis?   Tacet omne pecus, volucresque, feræque;

Et simulant fessos curvata cacumina somnos:

Nec trucibus fluviis idem sonus; occidit horror

Æquoris, et terris maria acclinata quiescunt.

Septima jam rediens Phœbe mihi respicit ægras

Stare genas; toties nostros Tithonia questus

Præterit, et gelido tangit miserata flagello.

Alme veni, nec te totas infundere pennas

Luminibus compello meis (hoc turba precetur

Lætior); extremo me tange cacumine virgæ

(Sufficit), aut levior suspenso poplite transi.

TO SLEEP.

Sleep, gentle sleep, what have I said or done,

That I alone, most miserable youth,

Call thee in vain?—All earth and air is still;

With bended heads the tree-tops feign repose;

The hoarse streams cease to murmur, and the sea

Leans its tired waves against the shore in rest.

Seven times the Moon returning has beheld

My wan and wakeful eyes; seven times the Dawn

Has pass'd with pity in her cold, grey beams.

Come, gentle God, I venture not to beg

Presumptuous the full shedding of thy wings—

Such prayers are for the happy—but for me

It were enough to feel thine extreme wand,

Or thy light presence pass on tip-toe by.

HADES.

Est via declivis funestâ nubila taxo :
ducit ad infernas per muta silentia sedes.
Styx nebulas exhalat iners : umbraeque recentes
descendunt illâc, simulacraque functa sepulcris.
Pallor Hiemsque tenent late loca senta : novique,
quà sit iter, manes, Stygiam quod ducat ad urbem,
ignorant : ubi sit nigri fera regia Ditis.
Mille capax aditus, et apertas undique portas
urbs habet.   Utque fretum de totâ flumina terrâ,
sic omnes animas locus accipit ille ; nec ulli
exiguus populo est, turbamve accedere sentit.
Errant exsangues sine corpore et ossibus umbrae ;
parsque forum celebrant, pars imi tecta tyranni ;
pars aliquas artes, antiquae imitamina vitae,
exercent : aliam partem sua poena coercet.

HADES.

A sloping road, obscured by funeral yews,
Leads through dumb silence to the realms of Death :
Dull Styx exhales in fog, and far and wide
Pallor and Winter have their dismal home :
And ghosts are seen, fresh from their sepulchres,
Journeying they know not whither ; ignorant
What road may lead to the grim battlements
Of Pluto, and the city of the dead.
Around the city's walls wideopen stand
A thousand gates ; and as into the sea
All rivers flow, so pours through every gate
The tide of spirits ; and the city still,
Tho' filling evermore, is never full.
Dim, spectral shapes, bloodless, incorporal,
Flit to and fro ; some in their shadowy homes
Linger ; some throng the forum and the street ;
And some their wonted occupations ply
In ghastly mimicry of bygone life ;
And some, a wretched crew, are doom'd to pay
The penalty of sin with endless woe.

INSCRIPTION FOR THE PEDESTAL OF
AN ATLAS TIME-PIECE.

A tiny ball of brass my load
    May seem to all beholders ;
They little think how huge a weight
    Is pressing on my shoulders.

For all the days in all the years,
    Each hour and every minute,
With Winter, Autumn, Summer, Spring,
    Lie cramm'd together in it.

ATLAS LOQUITUR.

Forsitan exiguam videor tibi tollere molem,

    Parvula nec pondus prodit imago suum.

Hic Vera, Æstates, Auctumni Hyemesque premuntur,

    Cumque suis horis Noxque Diesque latent.